# Everyone Goes to Heaven

# Everyone Goes to Heaven

Marina E. Michaels

Athena Star Press
athenastarpress.com

First edition April 2026
Library of Congress Control Number: 2026900658
Paperback: 978-1-60038-013-6
EPUB/Kindle: 978-1-60038-015-0

Paperback version printed in the United States of America with chlorine-free ink and on acid-free interior paper stock supplied by a provider certified by the Forest Stewardship Council.

Always and forever, to my beloved daughter, Elisabeth
without whom life would be so much poorer

## Acknowledgments

I appreciate beyond measure the folks who read an early version of this book and gave me invaluable feedback: Anita, Floyd, Frances, Jeff, Kenne, Linda, Paula, and Ren. Your comments and questions helped make this book clearer.

## Other Books by Marina E. Michaels

*The Forgiving Lifestyle: How to Forgive Everyone (Including Yourself)*

*Delectable Desserts* (volume 1 of the Delicious Connections cookbook series)

*Recipes Your Mother Knew by Heart* (volume 2 of the Delicious Connections cookbook series)

*A Distant Reality: Poems*

All available on Amazon worldwide

## Review request

Did this book help you in some way? If so, I'd love to hear about it through your review on Amazon, Goodreads, Barnes and Noble, or any other site. Honest reviews help readers find the right book for their needs.

## Praise from early readers

You are the real deal! I especially appreciate your emphasis on personal development; I don't think that's emphasized enough in spiritual groups. There's so much you've said in your book that is really important to say and which I haven't seen in New Age books. You've explained your approach to your mysticism using logic and reason! That's not a forte of New Age writing—that I've come across. —Anita P.

You have done an amazing job at compiling your knowledge and presenting it in an organized fashion that's easy to follow. — Paula M.

I thought the book was excellent. It was comprehensive, eye-opening to those who are willing to read what you present. Many of your writings also agree with what I've been told or shown, so I really hope that people can read the book with an open mind. It's what's needed! — Linda D..

# Contents

# Chapter 1
# We have nothing to fear from death

The ancient Egyptians believed in a goddess they called Ma'at. She personified truth, justice, responsibility, and integrity. When someone died, their heart was weighed on scales against Ma'at's feather, which represented those values. If the person's heart balanced with the feather, the person had lived life following those values, and was allowed to go on to the afterlife. If their heart didn't balance, meaning they had been dishonest, unjust, irresponsible, and lacked integrity, they were sent to the underworld.

*Figure 1. Ma'at's scale of justice weighs a human's heart—what kind of person that human was in life—against her feather of truth. The heart is in a jar on the left; the feather is on the right.*

This ancient belief, like beliefs across the world and throughout time, holds deep truths and a universal admonishment to always strive to be a better human being. Many cultures and religions teach these truths, and this weighing of the heart is close to what I have seen happen to the dearly departed in my many years as a psychic and medium.

This book contains stories from my experiences as a psychic and a medium. The book focuses on the afterlife and on what we can do now to prepare for it, and discusses related topics that are good to know more about both in this life and the next. I hope what I say reassures you that there is nothing to fear from death.

You may wonder why you should care about the afterlife. You might think what we do while in physical reality has nothing to do with what happens to us after bodily death, or you might think that somehow you will magically become a better soul after your body dies. From what I've seen, neither is the case. Who we are now is who we are in the afterlife. A good analogy is this: If you walk from one room of your home to another, do you expect to suddenly be a different person? Of course not. Just the same is true when you move from the land of the living into the afterlife. In the afterlife, we are exactly as we were. That's why it's so important to understand what the afterlife is like, why what we do now matters, and what we can do to prepare ourselves for the afterlife. And that's what this book is about.

What I describe is based on what I've seen and heard from people who have left their physical bodies and are now living elsewhere, mostly on what some call a different plane of existence. In that place, I have only ever seen infinite justice and mercy. I call that place heaven because what I see most closely matches that term. You might call it something else: Gan Eden, Helheim, Jannah, Paradise, Svargaloka, or another term. Whatever you want to call it is okay. Labels aren't nearly as important as the reality. For the most part, throughout this book, I refer to it as the afterlife because that term is factual and non-denominational. As you will see, the afterlife is infinitely variable and the dearly departed experience it in different ways depending on what they believe.

In this book, I reassure you that only good things await us after death. There is no hell. There is no punishment for the bad things we have done while in an earthly body. (Though we must acknowledge and learn from the bad things we did in life.) Because I'm all for people making up their own minds based on the information they receive, you don't need to believe anything I say. If you disagree with or dislike something in this book, trust yourself and stick by your guns. Maybe you're right; maybe I'm right. Maybe we are both right for different reasons. The most important thing is to be responsible to and for yourself and your beliefs, and to be respectful of others. We're all (well, most of us are) human beings, and most of us want to do the right thing.

As you read this book, you may notice that there is no "one size fits all" afterlife. Yes, we all go through the same stages in the afterlife, but how we go through those stages, and the decisions we make in those stages, and what the afterlife is like, are as unique and individual as we are. If what I say brings comfort and hope to you, I'll be happy.

In this book, you'll find many ideas that I haven't seen advanced by anyone else, and those ideas could be intriguing or challenging. Some are contrary to ideas that are commonly accepted in various groups, such as the idea that angels have free will. I believe they do; many others believe they don't. I explain why in chapter 4. Even if you don't agree with everything I say, I ask that you keep an open mind. As Hamlet says to his best friend in William Shakespeare's play *Hamlet*, "There are more things in Heaven and Earth, Horatio, than are dreamt of in your philosophy." The two friends were discussing their encounter with Hamlet's father's ghost, which Horatio was doubting. In my many decades of experience as a psychic, I've had my eyes opened to a number of things I once didn't think existed or that I believed operated differently, and I've written about some of those here. Even if what I say is new to you, what you read can help you both in this life and the next.

It sounds immodest for me to say this, so I generally don't: I'm the real deal. I've been told by a well-known psychic that I am a world-class psychic. Often, spiritual teachers are teaching theories based on something they read or were taught, not on direct experience. Unless I say otherwise, I've experienced everything I write about.

# Chapter 2
# Where do we go from here?

Everyone has their beliefs about life and death, about whether we *have* souls or *are* souls or are biological machines run by our genes, machines that vanish at bodily death.

What do you think you are? Do you believe, as Socrates did, that our earthly existence is an immortal soul inhabiting and running a mortal body? Or do you believe you "have" a soul as something separate from you, the person reading this book? Or do you believe you're here now, but that your existence will stop when your body stops working?

What do you think awaits us after our physical bodies stop working? Do you think you'll go to a place called heaven or hell or Valhalla or Fólkvangr (or any of the other Norse afterlife locations) or paradise or nirvana or the Celestial Kingdom or some other celestial realm, depending on your religion or beliefs? Do you think you'll be judged for everything you've done, good or bad? Do you think you'll be punished for everything you did wrong? Do you think there's nothing after bodily death and you'll vanish forever? Do you think you'll be absorbed into a vast silent sea of energy, dissolved into nothingness, and bereft of all individuality and of everything you've done? Do you think you'll be reborn, the same person as you are now? Do you think we are nothing but mechanical beings running around and controlled by our genes, which have nothing more in mind than to survive?

In his book, *The Power of Myth*, Joseph Campbell succinctly states the question in this manner: "What am I? Am I the bulb that carries the light? Or am I the light of which the bulb is a vehicle?" (Joseph Campbell and Bill Moyers, *The Power of Myth*, Doubleday, 1988.) He's saying that we aren't our bodies (the light bulb); instead, we are souls—the light—that inhabits our bodies. So many people talk about "having" a soul, but Campbell is saying we don't *have* souls, we *are* souls.

*Figure 2. In this image of two light bulbs, the bulbs represent our physical bodies. The light in the bulb on the right represents our souls, which create, move, and maintain our bodies. Without a soul, our bodies (the light bulb on the left) are lifeless. With a soul, our bodies are alive.*

We all believe things and are often certain that we are right and that those who disagree with us are wrong. Perhaps we need this certainty to feel safe and secure in this world. For if we allow that our beliefs are beliefs and not reality, and therefore possibly wrong, what then can we be sure of? And how can we feel good about ourselves if we are wrong about everything?

The answer is that all beliefs contain a kernel of truth within them. Maybe a lot, maybe not much, but truth nonetheless. The rest is influenced by who we are, our attitudes, our natural inclinations to be narrow or broad in our thinking, and by our culture, family, and friends.

And to a certain extent by our degree of honesty. The less honest and less courageous among us will ignore information that contradicts or alters our beliefs; the more rigorously honest among us aren't afraid of being wrong, and are more willing to acknowledge new information and incorporate it into our beliefs, modifying what we believe to more properly fit the facts as we now see them.

Whatever your beliefs about souls and the afterlife, I ask that you have an open mind as you read this book. Now, you might be wondering if I've had a near-death experience. Yes, I've had a few. My memories from those experiences are mildly interesting to me, but they're perhaps uninteresting to anyone else. The only relevant thing to say is that I never saw a tunnel of light. I don't have an opinion on people seeing a tunnel of light beyond that I think it's a symbolic representation of what's really happening. (I discuss the symbolic nature of our experiences in the greater reality in chapter 5.)

Instead, in this book I talk about my experiences as a psychic and medium talking with the dearly departed and receiving information from many non-physical sources. The information I've received is universally useful.

## *Immediately after bodily death*

Let's look at what I've seen of the afterlife when speaking with the dearly departed. In my experience, we are immortal souls inhabiting bodies. That means when our bodies die, that's not the end of us. After our bodies die, we as souls go through the following stages:

1. We leave our bodies and head for the afterlife, usually right away (with help—see the next section), but sometimes with a delay. This is perhaps one of the most important messages of this book: Everyone goes to heaven eventually. *When* they go is up to them; some people wait a while. One soul I know of still hasn't gone to the afterlife, and that soul has been on earth for quite a while now.
2. Once in heaven, we go through our life review. This usually takes place right away, but not always.
3. After the life review, we go to one of a few possible places depending on several factors. As I said, there is no "one size fits all" experience in the afterlife.

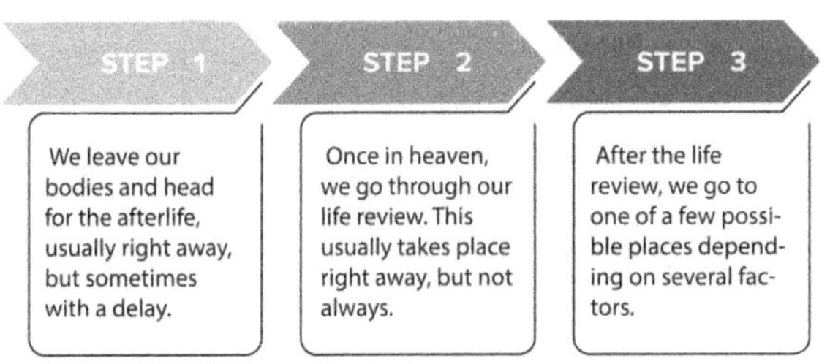


*Figure 3. After bodily death, we take steps toward the afterlife in stages.*

And to be very clear, there is no physical pain in the afterlife. Once we leave our physical bodies, all physical pain stops.

Chapter 3 covers in more detail what happens when we arrive in the afterlife. I describe what happens to those who remain on earth in chapter 13. As you read what we do after our bodily death, take what makes sense to you and set aside the rest.

## *How do we get to the afterlife?*

Explaining how we get to the afterlife means going into dimensional existence and how many realities are right here, layered on top of each other and interleaving with each other—most of us just don't see them and aren't aware of them. The super brief answer: We don't physically move once we're out of our physical bodies; instead, we change our perceptions so we see and are in another reality (or dimension if you prefer to use that term). The existence of multiple realities that are layered and interleaved among each other also explains how a skilled psychic can see the unseen.

Once a soul's body is dead, the soul is still alive. Depending on a person's beliefs when they were in a living body, after bodily death, they will perceive what's around them in different ways. (I mean what they truly believed, not what they told other people they believed.) For example, if they truly believed in an afterlife and truly believed that they were loved and cherished by the Divine, they may see a angels or beloved friends and relatives or other beloved souls (such as a beloved animal companion) waiting for them. Those beings will guide them to the afterlife.

If a person didn't truly believe in any of that, and instead either secretly believed there is no Divine being, nor is there infinite justice, love, and mercy waiting for them, or believed in eternal punishment, they may see nothing, or they may see frightening beings and images.

Many people will be in between these extremes. They'll realize they're still alive, but they aren't prepared for a non-physical reality and don't know how to move around in that non-physical reality. Sometimes they don't realize their bodies are dead—I go into more detail on that in chapter 13. Yet even if they realize their bodies are dead, they may not see the help that is waiting there to guide them to the afterlife. They may, however, be open to seeing a psychopomp—a being who specializes in escorting souls from their now-dead bodies to the afterlife. Often a psychopomp is a soul still in a living body who is volunteering to help such people.

Until I gave birth to my daughter, I acted as a psychopomp for years, never knowing exactly how or why I ended up with that job. After I gave birth, I was no longer asked to do that job; I think because it wasn't safe for a newly arrived soul (my daughter) to be exposed to souls leaving physical reality, because the temptation to possess the newborn's body might be too much for some souls.

The psychopomp is assigned a group of people (for me, it was seldom a single soul, but usually many at a time). The psychopomp then leads those souls on what looks like a journey through strange landscapes that are partly physical looking and partly surreal and Dali-esque. (Salvador Dali was a Spanish artist who painted things like melting watches. Look him up if you're interested.)

This journey isn't physical—it's in the spirit realm. So what seems to be physical travel is simply moving through nonphysical thought forms and beliefs. As the souls travel, guided by the psychopomp, they are also moving away from beliefs in physical-reality constructs and more deeply into the constructs of what I call the greater reality. In a sense, they aren't moving at all; they are changing their perspectives and therefore their perceptions. Eventually they cover enough nonphysical "ground" to arrive in the afterlife, where they are guided (not by the psychopomp) to begin their life review.

The takeaway here is that nobody is left behind; help is always there. And although those of us left in the physical realm grieve for those who have moved on, those who have moved on can now be filled with joy.

## *Do we change when we go to the afterlife?*

One misunderstanding (or maybe it's a hope) some people have is that when they reach the afterlife, they will be purged of all their flaws and will instantly become an enlightened being. You're a greedy, vicious, soul-sucking person in life? No worries! In the afterlife, you're sure you'll instantly become generous, gentle, and kind, so do what you want now and to heck with consequences. Such people believe that none of those consequences matter because the slate will be wiped clean. Aleister Crowley's often-misinterpreted quote ("Do what thou wilt"), which is used by many as permission and justification to do anything we want regardless of any harm we're inflicting on ourselves or others, is an example of this destructive belief.

Alas, this is not the case. As I said in chapter 1, we don't miraculously become better souls immediately upon bodily death. We don't change one bit, at least not at first. Moving to the afterlife is like moving from one room of our house to another: We are exactly the same person, we're just now in a new location. Just as we don't change when we walk from one room of our home into another, whatever we've made of ourselves while in a human body is what we are after bodily death. In the afterlife, we can learn and grow and become better souls, but only if we want to, and only through our own efforts. If we want to become better, we have to work on ourselves. Nobody is going to wave a magic wand and make all the bad things go away. The good news is, we don't have to wait until our bodies die to start becoming a better soul. I talk a lot more about this in chapter 12.

Likewise, our relationships remain the same. If we love someone while in a physical body, we still love them in the afterlife. Conversely, if we hated someone while in a physical body, we still hate them in the afterlife. Yes, we still have emotions in the afterlife. I talk more about that in chapter 6.

Are you curious about what I mean by "at least, not at first"? I mean we don't change right away. We can continue to grow and change, and most of us do. Often when contacting someone's dearly departed who has been in the afterlife for a long time, that person has changed enough that my client might not recognize them if they presented themselves as they are now. So instead, they present themselves as they were when in a physical body. That way, as I describe the dearly departed's personality, the client recognizes that I am genuinely speaking with the dearly departed. As the session continues, the dearly departed then starts to show how they've changed. It's heartwarming and reassuring to know that we can all become better souls in the afterlife.

## *What is the afterlife like?*

Your first question to someone who has seen the afterlife might be, "What is the afterlife like?"

I've said it's a place of infinite justice and mercy, and I've said everyone goes there, but I haven't given specifics.

The first thing to know is this: The afterlife *looks* like physical reality, but it's a malleable, non-physical place where thoughts and intentions are more immediately powerful. By "malleable," I mean the substance of the afterlife is responsive to our thoughts and wishes. By "more immediately powerful," I mean that while our thoughts and intentions are powerful on the earthly plane, they are enormously more powerful in the afterlife. Our beliefs affect what we see as well, which is why you hear sometimes conflicting stories about what the afterlife is like from people who have visited it and returned to physical reality.

If you've seen the 1998 movie, *What Dreams May Come*, you have a glimpse of what the afterlife can look like, with these exceptions: the afterlife doesn't have a place to punish people, people who committed suicide aren't segregated and punished, and I haven't seen the afterlife looking like a living painting. I'm not excluding the possibility that some parts of the afterlife could look like that; I just haven't seen them when speaking to the dearly departed. As Jesus said, "In the home of my father there are many abodes." (John 14:2, Ferrar Fenton translation.) I take this to mean that how the afterlife appears to us is infinitely variable according to our beliefs and needs.

The afterlife is a glorious place where everyone is safe and free. No more pain, no more abuse, no more misunderstandings, no more hatred or prejudice or anything other than freedom and love. Yet although there is no pain in the afterlife, there can be all other emotions, both what we consider good and bad.

No one is punished in the afterlife, though some people are kept separate in what I see as a special school. Suicide is a mistake, but it's not punished. I talk about the school later in this chapter and in chapter 3, and about suicide in chapter 9.

In the afterlife, you have a body that, like the afterlife itself, looks physical, but isn't. You can move from place to place in the afterlife, but instead of using physical effort, you use thought, intention, and desire as the motivating force. If you want to be in a redwood forest, you feel that desire and you instantly are there in a heavenly redwood forest. If you want to spend time at a beach, there you are on a heavenly beach. If you want to ski, you are on a heavenly ski slope. Love golf? No worries. There you are on a heavenly golf course in, if you wish, a heavenly golf cart.

*Figure 4. The heavenly realm can contain any type of environment and location.*

But don't think this heavenly existence is a reason to exit life early! In chapter 9, I talk about how suicide is one of the biggest mistakes anyone can make; every person I've spoken with in the afterlife who took themselves out of physical life has expressed profound regret at that decision. They often did it because they thought they could come back and do it again, and only found out too late that that's not how it works.

Personality wise, in the afterlife we are who we were in life, with one exception, an exception I won't go into because it's not relevant to understanding what the afterlife is and isn't. If we were kind in life, we're still kind in the afterlife. If we weren't a good person in life, we don't suddenly become a good person in the afterlife. A person with the soul of a poisonous snake doesn't become a saint when they die.

This is an overview of the afterlife's mechanics; in a bit, I talk more specifically about what we experience in the afterlife.

## *The afterlife is what you want it to be*

We experience the spirit realm through symbols; therefore what *I* see and what *you* see can vary widely, though the underlying truth is the same. (You'll find more information on symbols in chapter 5.) Keep this in mind as I describe what I've seen. And because the afterlife is what you want it to be, no specific description of the afterlife is complete or completely accurate. Everyone who has genuinely experienced the afterlife (for example, in a near-death experience, when their physical body died and their souls temporarily escaped, only to return to their bodies), has experienced a different version of the afterlife according to who they are and what they believed.

This is why you'll hear varying accounts from people returning from a near-death experience. We experience the afterlife according to our needs, beliefs, expectations, preferences, and religion. If someone is a Christian, they will have experienced the afterlife as some version of the Christian heaven and will have reported what they saw according to those beliefs. If they're a Pagan, they might have experienced the afterlife as a Pagan place—Helheim, for example, or some other such place.

Which leads to a brief discussion of what the afterlife is called. Christians call the afterlife Heaven. In other religions, the afterlife is variously called Gan Eden, Helheim, Jannah, Paradise, Svargaloka, and so on,. Whatever you believe about the afterlife, that's what you'll experience when you arrive. All this occurs after you go through your life review, that is, and if you weren't sent to the special school I write of in chapter 3.

All those experiences are true and real. No beliefs except one contradict any other beliefs about the afterlife. The one belief that many share but that isn't true in any of the realities and versions of the afterlife I've seen is the belief in hell or some form of punishment. There is no hell; at least, I've never seen it, and I've seen a lot of extra-physical places, psychically speaking. I go into more detail on hell in chapter 7. (Hell isn't the same as the Norse afterlife location called Helheim, ruled by Hel, Loki's daughter. Although the names look similar and sound alike, Helheim is very different from the Christian concept of hell. In fact, Helheim is similar to the heaven I describe in this book.)

Let's look at some of the sights of the afterlife I've seen through the eyes of the dearly departed. As I describe my experiences, you might want to refer to my analogy of the map versus the territory, which I describe in appendix A. To summarize, what we see of existence is our individual *map* of reality, it isn't reality itself. Also, what Dante says in *Paradiso*, Canto XXIX, line 12 (the Dorothy Sayers translation), "every *where* and every *when*" centers in the afterlife.

I received one of my first glimpses of the afterlife in my early years as a practicing psychic when a friend, Jeff Duntemann, asked about his departed father. I saw his father in a Swiss ski chalet in the Alps. He was sitting in a cozy wooden alcove at a thick wooden table, lifting steins with a group of friends. Jeff said that sounded like his father. (Jeff has given his permission to share the story and his name.)

## *Dante's weird take on heaven and hell*

I think Dante had a lot of things right, and did a decent job of interpreting and portraying his beliefs. As an interesting take on hell, he portrayed people as being in hell for two reasons: Either those people lived before the time of Christ, and therefore weren't redeemed when Christ did his thing on the cross, or they are in hell because they are unrepentant of the harmful deeds they did when alive. Once they repent, they can move on to heaven.

The first reason always puzzled me. Why couldn't the power of Christ stretch backward to the past as easily as it affects the future? The only answer I have is that Dante's conception of time was as a linear, forward-moving force, not as simultaneous. The second reason—that people remain in hell because they aren't ready to repent of their bad actions—makes more sense and is in line with what I see as happening in the special school.

## *The heavenly golf course*

You may be wondering why I used a golf course to illustrate one of the many ways the afterlife appears to us. There's a story behind that. After I'd been practicing as a psychic for closing in on a decade, I met Linda Derose-Droubay, who became a lifelong friend. I had just started working at Next Level Communications, a telecom company that later bit the dust. My husband at the time, who also worked at the company, introduced Linda and me. When I meet people, I don't usually lead with "I'm a psychic," but during Linda's and my first conversation, my intuition told me to tell Linda that I was psychic.

Her reaction was neutrally polite, but I'd started her thinking.

About two hours after we met, she came to my cubicle and asked if she could ask about her father, who had recently died. I said "yes."

A reassurance: I've gotten permission from Linda to tell this story, but most of the answers I received for Linda were personal, so I don't repeat them here. One of my ethical standards as a psychic and human being is "Never without permission." I always ask permission to communicate psychically with anyone and anything. I ask permission of the living, I ask permission of the souls of living people who aren't close enough to ask in person, and I ask permission of souls who have moved on from physical reality. I also never share a client's private information with anyone—that's a violation of boundaries and their trust. It's their information and they can share it if they wish; it's not mine to share without permission.

You might think that if I'm asking souls psychically for permission, I must always be granted that permission. That might be the case if I were making it all up or if I were self-deluded enough to not be able to hear the truth, but that isn't the case. Sometimes when I approach people on the soul level, I am refused permission. Sometimes the soul wants to listen to me continue with my psychic reading with a client, and then they decide to trust me and say yes. Sometimes I get a flat "no" that never changes. I take the fact that I am sometimes refused permission as a confirmation that I'm not making up the permissions I receive; therefore I am more likely to trust it when I hear a "yes."

After receiving permission from Linda's father to communicate with him, I saw him seated on a golf cart on an enormous golf course. The golf course stretched in all directions, with some mountains in the far distance.

I told Linda what I saw, and told her the answers her father was giving me to pass along to her. She had some concerns that I was able to reassure her about based on what her father was telling me.

Surprised, Linda said her father loved golfing, and that my answers were reassuring.

The point of this story is not that I was accurate about Linda's father; the point is that he loved golfing, so he was golfing in the afterlife. If he had loved horseback riding, he might have been riding horses. If he loved fishing, he might have been fishing. Whatever you love doing, you can do in the afterlife. That doesn't mean you'll golf eternally; you may spend some time golfing, some time visiting with friends and family, and some time doing other things that bring you joy.

I've never seen people in the afterlife floating around on clouds playing harps. Though perhaps the people I've spoken with had already done their harp thing and just didn't mention it. If you want to float around on clouds playing a harp in the afterlife, you can totally do that.

Of all the views of the afterlife I've seen through the eyes of the dearly departed, although I've seen the dearly departed joyfully working on many heavenly projects, I've never seen anyone slaving away in a corporate office, or in any other sort of work for the sake of making money. There's nothing wrong with money—it's a neutral, simple representation of units of exchange and is useful in physical reality. It's just not needed in the afterlife.

Earth is a different matter. The older I get, the truer this Biblical statement is to me: "For the love of money is the root of all these evils." (1 Timothy 6:10, Ferrar Fenton translation). In the context of this Biblical quote, if someone loves money more than anything else, above all human considerations, they will do all manner of evil to get that money. Most people misquote this as "Money is the root of all evil," which completely misses the point. Though it furthers the agenda of making poverty seem pious.

## *Spirit communications—not everyone's equipment is online*

After I answered Linda's questions, she asked me why I could hear her father and she couldn't. After all, I'd never met him, and he was her father. Why hadn't her father tried to communicate with her?

I answered her question with this analogy. Imagine we all have smart phones in our minds. We use those phones to communicate with other souls, both in and outside physical reality.

Now imagine that some people have their phones on "do not disturb," or the ringers turned off, or the volume turned down so low, they can't hear their phones ring. And further imagine that many people locked their phones, then forgot their unlock code, so they can neither make nor receive calls even if they wanted to. Others may have their phones unlocked, but they've been invalidated so often by others that they no longer trust themselves and think they're imagining the ringing they hear. And even if someone answers a call (usually in a dream, but sometimes while awake), they dismiss the communication and tell themselves they're making it up, or tell themselves it was "just a dream," as though dreams can't bring us true information. Or, if they share their experience, they are invalidated and convinced by others that they were wrong.

Everyone has a psychic phone. That ability is built in and nothing can take it away. It's like in Golden Earring's 1973 song *Radar Love*. None of us needs a physical device to communicate; we can all communicate psychically with each other and with non-corporeal beings. But we aren't all using our phones to their fullest capabilities, or at all. For some people, using our psychic phones comes naturally; others need training. And many of us were invalidated when we were children and forgot we have the psychic phone, or even no longer believe in that form of communication, or were taught that psychically received information is all lies fed to us by the devil. (I sometimes wonder how this attitude can live side-by-side with the records of the Biblical prophets. Do such people believe only the prophets could get divinely inspired messages?) I'm working on a manuscript that teaches everything you need to know to revitalize and further develop your psychic abilities, but that's not this book's topic.

So what's a soul to do if they want to communicate with someone? They keep calling different "phones" until they reach someone who can answer. In most cases, that's someone like me: a sensitive or psychic. And that's what I told Linda.

## *Heavenly projects*

I mentioned heavenly projects. By that I mean projects people take on in the afterlife. The afterlife is infinite and allows for infinite variety and infinite experiences. I've seen many kinds of projects. Most of them are vast group projects that are being created to help the earth. Hosts of beings are working on those projects—not just souls who lived a life as a human, but other types of souls as well: angels and other highly evolved souls.

Most of these projects are to help those of us still in physical reality on this planet, not just we humans, but every living being on the planet. (There may be other, off-world projects, but if there are, none of the dearly departed I've spoken with are working on such.) None of these projects is mandatory. Only those who wish to are working on them.

One such project many folks in the afterlife are creating is a new set of thought structures for those of us on earth to use. These thought structures will help us to shift more easily away from old fear-based thoughts of competition, coercion, controlling others, and so on, to new thoughts of cooperation, compassion, and understanding, so we can more easily become better human beings, making the planet a better place to live. These structures are being gradually introduced worldwide.

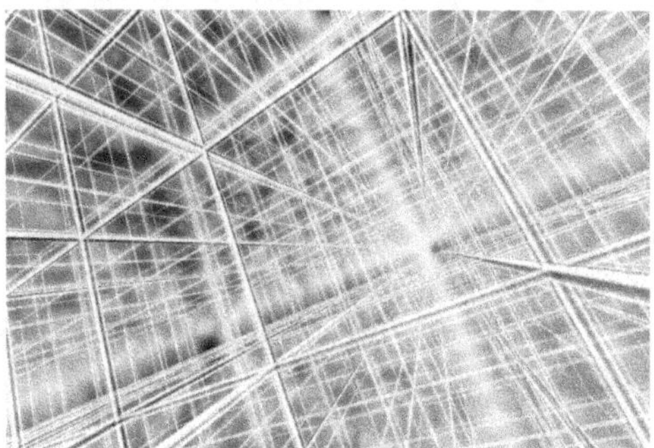

*Figure 5. A rough, approximate representation of a thought structure. This image also represents us as we are in multiple dimensions.*

Another project is devoted to creating energetic structures to support and help the natural world. That makes sense because we humans are part of that world, and the natural world and its inhabitants are valued, beloved, essential, indispensable parts of existence just as we humans are.

Some projects are smaller and more individual—helping family still on earth, for example.

The people in the afterlife whom I've spoken with, those who are working on any of these projects, express joy and fulfillment at being involved. They don't work on the projects 24/7, not that time is a constraint in the afterlife anyway. Instead, they work on projects when they wish, and they also visit people in the afterlife and do whatever fun things they want to do.

# Chapter 3
# What happens when we arrive in the afterlife?

Now that we've talked about what the afterlife is like, the next question is, what happens when we first arrive there?

For most people, the first thing we do when we get to the afterlife is go through what many call the life review—a minute-by-minute recounting of everything a person experienced, did, and thought while in physical life. Although I'd heard other people talking about the life review, I didn't believe in it until I accidentally dropped in on a tiny section of my mother's life review shortly after her death in 2002. Sure enough, she was recounting everything she'd done in chronological order. That convinced me that we do a life review as a first action in the afterlife.

## *Our first task in the afterlife: The life review*

I've only seen that one life review, so I can't say for sure, but I believe what the life review location looks like varies according to the person going through it. When I dropped in on my mother's life review, she was sitting on a comfortable brown leather couch in an office. The person she was talking to was to my left, around a corner and therefore not in my sight, though I got the impression they were sitting at a large oaken desk by some heavy oak bookcases filled with books. To my mother's right (at the far wall of the office) was a large window. Outside the window was a meadow filled with tall grasses and wildflowers, with a pine forest at the further edge. Deer grazed the meadow near the forest. (I've since psychically seen this meadow in other contexts.)

*Figure 6. One way the life review can appear is as a counselor's office. Your mileage may vary depending on your expectations and beliefs.*

My mother was comfortable and sounded happy. She was telling a minute-by-minute story of something that happened before I was born, when she was still married to my biological father and only had my three older brothers, Norm, David, and Pete. I got the impression that she'd been narrating the story of her life, that I'd dropped in on just one moment of that narration, and that she was going to continue her narration until she told everything to the moment of her bodily death. I also got the impression that she thought she was still in a physical body and was in a counselor's office in physical life.

I only stayed a moment; as soon as I realized what I was seeing, I left.

After that, I never saw or heard anyone else's life review. I think I was allowed to witness that tiny bit of her life review so I could know that the life review exists and a bit about what it's like. Since then, I've received more information related to the life review.

1. The life review is mandatory, but we get to decide when to do it. We can delay it forever if we wish. We just can't move on to the next stage in our existence until we do our life review.
2. The life review is a minute-by-minute recounting of everything we did, thought, said, and experienced in life. Everything. We have total recall. Denial is no longer possible. We can no longer pretend to ourselves that we didn't do something.

3. We aren't judged during or after our life review. There's someone there listening, but they are compassionate, kind, and loving. We are safe, and we know we're safe.
4. We can take however much time we wish in our life review, though from our perspective on earth, once a person starts their life review, it takes six months to a year for that person to complete the process.
5. People can't be interrupted during their life review. As a medium, I can sometimes get messages to, from, or about someone who is still going through their life review, but only with special permission, and only short messages until they're done with their life review.
6. For the most part, the life review is often simply a recounting of our life, not an analysis session; we don't start thinking about what happened in our life, or healing from those events, until after we've recounted all our memories. However, there is no one rule; what happens in our life review depends on our life experiences.

In a psychic reading, I saw that the client's dearly departed, although in the afterlife, was still convinced she was alive in a physical body, despite being told that she no longer had a physical body. As I said earlier, the afterlife *looks* physical, but is entirely energy that responds to our thoughts. Once a soul arrives in the afterlife, they still look to themselves however they believe they should look. In this woman's case, she looked to herself as she had looked in a physical body, and was having a hard time changing her beliefs, because the afterlife wasn't what she expected. She was a trifle stubborn; therefore, rather than change her mind, she insisted to herself and those around her that she was still alive in a physical body. Because she wasn't acknowledging her bodily death, and because she was refusing to acknowledge anything else going on around her, she was refusing to start her life review. In such cases, it takes a bit of convincing for a person to accept that they've left the physical plane. In her case, when she accepts that, she'll be ready for her life review.

## *What happens when we need healing?*

In February 2024, I psychically asked my non-physical contacts what happens in the afterlife to people who need emotional and mental healing. I received a message with more details on the life review process. In summary, the answer was that all physical ailments, having only been a part of our physical life, are gone completely once we leave our physical bodies. But emotional and mental trauma stays with us, since they affect our souls and our souls are who we are. Therefore we need to heal from those traumatic events in the afterlife. The following material (between the three stars) is the more detailed answer I received. The wording is as it was given to me. I lightly edited the material to make some of the phrasing more understandable. I've added clarifying information in brackets.

* * *

*The first thing you need to know is that everyone is healed once they come to the afterlife. [That is, we all go through a healing process as needed.] No one needs to know the details of anyone's healing. There is no one process by which someone is healed, nor is there a time line. It is all individual. It is all tailored to the person and their needs.*

*For example, when some people are doing their life review, they can be assisted in working through light trauma. If they experienced trauma only once or a few times in their life, they are helped in their life review to move through that trauma.*

*For those who experienced multiple traumas, or lifelong trauma, they need more help, help that cannot be accommodated in the life review. Instead, during the life review, light traumas, one-off occurrences from which they took harm, and experiences at that lighter level of pain and anguish are dealt with. Then processes are set in place for longer-term healing for deeper pain to take place after the life review.*

*Your physical life gives you all that you need. You are given all that you need to heal, all you need to learn, all that you need to live a joyful, fulfilled life. That help is always there. It is unfortunate that human society is not yet geared toward teaching people to recognize the help that is there. People aren't taught to be introspective, to be self-aware, and to be self-responsible.*

*Human society is evolving toward that kind of teaching; toward teaching children from infancy that they are loved, they are wanted, they are precious and irreplaceable, and toward teaching children from infancy to be autonomous and self-actualizing. One day, humans will reach that level of self-awareness and love for themselves and each other. Many of the heavenly projects you have written of are geared toward helping humanity reach that day. [Here, they are talking about what I say earlier in this book.]*

*But for now, for those who were not unconditionally loved as children, and who might even have been hated through their childhood, once they reach the afterlife, they get the help they needed in life.*

*Now, many people were and are inherently more highly responsible than others. Those people take responsibility for their own healing while in physical life. They seek help. They are more open to seeing help, even when that help seems unconventional, or is obscured, or is otherwise hard to recognize as help. These people sometimes miss the signs and clues [of that help], but not all, and therefore as they live their lives, they grow, and they heal themselves.*

*But what, you ask, of those who were less responsible in life? What of those who believed they were victims and had no choice? The answer is a bit more complicated. A certain percentage of believing you're a victim comes from how you were raised. A certain percentage is the kind of person you chose to be in this life. That type of person is determined by the decisions that you and the greater soul you are a part of decided before you broke off from your greater soul and chose to be born in a human body. Your greater soul could be exploring certain questions, such as "what is life like if you decide to live it thinking you are a victim?" Now we will say that all greater souls do that kind of exploration as they send their various aspects into physical reality. And when people talk about past lives, they are in fact talking about other aspects of their greater soul that they are closest to in terms of the explorations that the greater soul is doing throughout space and time. [See chapter 8 for a description of my take on reincarnation and what the being who was answering my question about healing is talking about in this paragraph.]*

*And here it gets even more complicated. What each of those selves is learning is shared by both the greater soul from which they came and by all the other selves sent out into physical reality [by the greater soul]. And cumulatively all that learning informs, is shared by, the greater soul. And in that sense, in that way the greater soul grows and evolves. In another sense, you could say that the end point of that greater soul already exists in its entirety. And therefore you could say that the greater self already knew everything all the selves learned. And yet there is a progression, there is a forward movement, there is an evolution from, you might say, a beginner soul to a mature, evolved soul.*

*Let's return to the state of a soul who reached the afterlife without believing in their own ability to be responsible for themselves. Those souls are not tossed to the wolves. That would not be a loving or responsible thing to do on the part of those responsible for running and governing the afterlife.*

*Instead, those souls are given what they need, in the form they need it, in a way that they can accept it. If, for example, a soul needs light healing, then much of that healing is accomplished during the life review, and any remaining healing that is needed is accomplished while they are enjoying the afterlife.*

*If they were more deeply traumatized, more deeply harmed, their healing is tailored to what they need. If they were so deeply harmed that they can't enjoy the afterlife, then they are sent to what you would call a special healing place, where that place is tailored to their unique needs. If they can enjoy the afterlife, they might go to the greater area of the afterlife, the common area of the afterlife if you will, where they can continue their healing with special helpers while they otherwise go about enjoying the afterlife.*

*So as you see, as we said earlier, there is no one-size-fits-all response to a soul's needs. If you want to say all this in your book, you may. If you prefer, you can abbreviate what we have said.*

* * *

This is the end of the message I received, which was from a combination of three beings: Metatron, the god/goddess of the entirety of all existence, and Jesus. Metatron is in charge of the entirety of physical reality and is called the voice for God.

## The three paths after the life review

As Metatron et al. just said, after a person completes their life review, they are given what they need, in the form they need it, in a way that they can accept. One of three things happen:

1. They are released into the broad expanse of the afterlife.

2. They are sent to a special place where they can heal from severe trauma, or
3. They are sent to the special school to learn how to be better souls, which also includes healing from those experiences that caused them to choose to be not-so-good human beings.

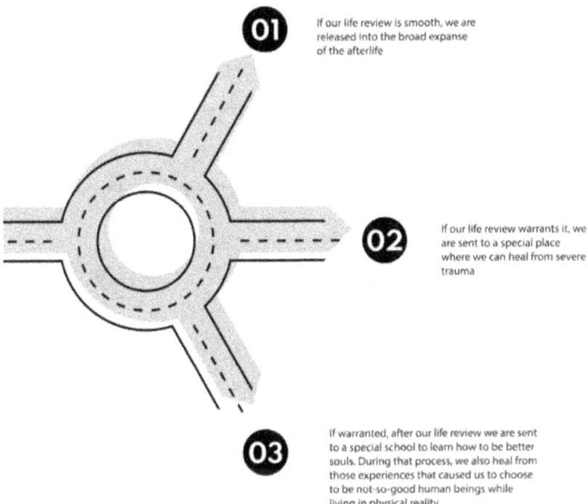


*Figure 7. The three paths after the life review depend on our soul's state.*

Why these differences? Because we don't suddenly become loving, enlightened, evolved people when we leave our bodies. We are in the afterlife who we were in life. If we were gentle and kind in life, we're still gentle and kind in the afterlife. If we were responsible, respectful people in life, we're still responsible and respectful in the afterlife. If we were abusive in life, we're still abusive in the afterlife. If we were a narcissist in life, we're still a narcissist in the afterlife, the main difference being that we can no longer deny our choices and their consequences. If we were abused and emotionally injured in life, we're still emotionally scarred in the afterlife. We aren't suddenly healed of all that pain when we enter the afterlife.

The difference between being an abusive person in life versus in the afterlife is that we don't get to get away with being abusive to others in the afterlife—in fact, it's impossible to harm others in the afterlife—and we can no longer deny our actions. (I'm convinced that if people didn't deny the things they've done, they would become better people, if only because they couldn't bear accepting that they are cruel or hateful to others.) But we can still justify our actions, both on earth and in afterlife. Once in the afterlife, we must face and acknowledge our bad actions toward others, and we can start working on learning to be more responsible.

If you're getting the idea that there's no one course of action in the afterlife, and that instead what happens depends on a variety of circumstances, you're right. That makes sense, because we are all individuals; none of us is exactly the same, and there's no reason for the Divine to treat us as though we were. Eventually, if you wish, you can leave the afterlife to go on to other adventures.

Let's look at the three paths people take once they arrive in the afterlife.

### ***Running free in the afterlife***

The easiest path to describe is when a soul has been responsible enough to be allowed free reign in the afterlife after their life review. If a soul completes their life review and needs neither deep healing (for example, if they received the light healing they needed during their life review), and aren't so harmful they need to be taught to be a better soul, they can run free in the afterlife immediately after their life review, without going for further healing or stopping in the special school. Once released, we can do what we wish as described in chapter 2.

### ***The healing place***

The middle case is for people who need deep healing. Just as we don't instantly become an enlightened, responsible being in the afterlife, we also aren't instantly healed of the emotional pain and trauma we suffered when in a physical body. If, for example, a soul needs only a light amount of healing, then much of that healing is accomplished during the life review, and any remaining healing that is needed is accomplished while they are enjoying the afterlife.

If they were more deeply harmed, and that soul doesn't need to go to the special school, they receive healing tailored to what they need. If they were so deeply harmed that they can't enjoy the afterlife (because they've lost all trust in others, and have lost all belief in anything good being possible for them), then they are sent to a special healing place, a place tailored to their unique needs. Eventually they heal enough to be able to enjoy the afterlife.

Then they go to the greater area of the afterlife, the common area if you will, where they can continue their healing with special helpers while they otherwise go about enjoying the afterlife.

I've psychically received a lot more information on this topic, but it gets complicated and isn't needed for this book. Just know that nothing is forever and that you can and will be completely healed in the afterlife.

## *The special school—a place for learning to be a better being*

The third case requires a lot more explanation. After their life review, if someone was a terrible and irresponsible human being in life, they aren't allowed to roam heaven freely until they learn to be better souls. They aren't punished—punishment would be the opposite of helpful. But they do need to learn how to be more responsible, and to learn why they should be more responsible, so they can rehabilitate and start to become better beings.

To learn these things, they are sent to a special school. There, they can no longer harm others. You could think of the special school as a place where souls can do the homework (the inner self-improvement work) they could and should have been doing in life. They also receive the healing needed to help them become better souls. In this section, I describe this place in more detail than I did the other two options. Why? Because if you know what's coming, you can make choices now, while you're in a physical body, that can help you avoid going to that special school. That is, assuming you aren't so deeply in denial about yourself that it isn't possible for you to see the need to be a better human being.

Not that there's anything wrong with the special school or with attending it, but you have a one-time-only opportunity now, while you are in a physical body, to do the work needed to avoid that special school in the afterlife. It's a waste of your time and energy to stay in denial while in a human body, and to therefore avoid making something better of yourself. You must do the work eventually; why not start now? It's not too late.

There's one exception: because of the reasons that caused narcissists to choose to be narcissists, they in particular are incapable of seeing the truth about themselves and so end up in the special school where they can learn to be better souls.

The special school is a gentle place where you are given all the time you need to fix yourself and your mistakes of thinking. But it's not a place of castigation; instead, you work on making yourself a better person in much the same way you could have done while on earth. You work on errors in thinking (about yourself and toward others) and start to heal from your own trauma that, when on earth, you decided to turn into blame for and attack of others.

*Figure 8. As with the life review location, the special school's appearance can change according to your expectations and beliefs.*

As I've learned more about Christian theology, I've come to think the special school is what Dante describes as purgatory in his *Purgatory* (the second of the three books in Dante's *The Divine Comedy*). "Special school" is my term for it; it sounds better and gives people more agency to call it a school than to call it purgatory, which has the negative connotation of being someplace outside heaven where you passively suffer and wait your turn to go to heaven. And it fits Dante's description of purgatory quite closely.

A lot of people are surprised to hear that Dante describes purgatory as being inside heaven. According to Dante, it's the first place everyone goes when they arrive in heaven. In purgatory, they purge themselves of all their inner wrongness (sins, according to Dante) before they can emerge into heaven proper.

In *The Divine Comedy*, you move into purgatory as soon as you decide to leave hell. (Dante says in *The Inferno*, the first book of his *Divine Comedy*, that the only people in hell are those who want to be there. As soon as they decide to repent, they are free to move on to purgatory.) According to Dante, you move through purgatory, purging yourself of all your sins, before you're ready to enter the main part of heaven. (Purgatory isn't in the Hebrew or Christian Bible, though medievalists thought something like it existed. The place was called the "limbo of the Fathers.")

Dante describes purgatory as a joyous place where people willingly go through the pain of purging themselves of their sins because they know the next step is to fully enter heaven. Other religions have a similar concept—that of people going to some temporary place to purify themselves of their earthly sins.

Let's take a closer look at the word "sin." In Mark Horn's excellent book, *Tarot and the Gates of Light* (Destiny Books, 2020), he says that the Hebrew word that is commonly translated as "sin" is more accurately translated as "mistake."

Does that make a difference to you? It does to me; it lightens the heaviness of the word sin, which is laden with millennia of judgment, punishment, and unforgiveness. In most religions, a sin is an irrevocable blot on our existence, a stain we can never wash out. Sinning makes you a horrible person, even an irredeemable person in some religions. So we double down and continue to sin because we see no redemption for ourselves.

But unlike sins, mistakes can be corrected. If we take a wrong turn while driving, we can always get back on our desired road by making the proper course corrections and changes. No matter how bad the mistake, you can do your best to make amends. Sometimes the best thing you can do is sincerely apologize. However, although an apology might help, it can't undo the harm you did. Also, if making amends is a new idea to you, know that sometimes you just cannot make amends to the person you harmed in this life.

Consider this analogy: Take a precious porcelain plate and smash it to the ground as hard as you can. That plate might be reparable with hours of patience and glue, but it will never be the same. In just the same way, when you harm someone, whether physically or emotionally, they will never completely heal from the harm. Even if you "only" harm them physically, the emotional and mental harm, including the pain from your betrayal and loss of trust for you, will never completely heal. This is especially true for abused children.

Some mistakes are truly, truly horrible and coming back from them takes time, sometimes a lot of time. And maybe not until you die and go to heaven (whatever you want to call it) can you recover from those mistakes. And you *will* go to heaven no matter what.

The point I hope you take from this discussion is that, even if you are harming others, you can decide that you want to be and do better and that you will start doing so right now. And if you are a generally kind and gentle person, you understand how valuable those traits are in the here and now.

## *School attendance is mandatory; the curriculum is responsibility*

If a soul is sent to the special school, attendance is mandatory and the soul must stay there until they learn what they need to learn. If they were instead allowed to run free in heaven, because heaven is malleable and responsive to our thoughts and intentions, they would do a lot of damage as they lashed out at others rather than controlling themselves.

In the special school, people are educated in becoming more responsible. They aren't forced to do or think anything, and they aren't spoon-fed the answers. They must find their answers themselves. They are shown gently and compassionately why responsibility is important, and they are taught how to start working on becoming better beings. If they are willing to do the work (and some aren't), they begin to discover their answers and make themselves better, less harmful souls. Until they learn enough to no longer be a danger to others, they are kept apart so they don't harm others in the afterlife.

We all need to learn these things not just to learn not to harm others, but also because, until we do, we can't evolve and grow as a soul, and therefore we can't keep moving forward through the adventure of the afterlife and beyond.

As a lifelong advocate of the power and importance of love, when I first learned of the special school, I was surprised to see that responsibility is the paramount skill to learn and develop. I would have expected the big lesson to be love. But after seeing why people are in the special school, and after thinking about the nature of emotions, love especially, I realized it makes sense for people to instead be taught responsibility. Why? Because

1. You can't force anyone to feel any emotions toward others, including love, and anyway
2. being responsible for yourself and toward others is a deep form of love.

In short, responsibility and respect, not love, make the world go round. In the special school, why are we not given lessons in loving each other? The answer is that an irresponsible person blames others for their choices and condition, saying that other people "made them" do or feel something, or saying they never had any choice but to take harmful actions, or waiting passively for some miracle—the next pill, the next surgery, something, anyone who promises relief—to come along and change their life circumstances. They don't change this attitude in heaven—not without help, that is. So they are still stuck in victim mode. But there is always a choice, and there's always help available, both seen and unseen.

But just as you can't make anyone feel emotions, it's impossible to make someone feel love toward someone. Responsibility, on the other hand, is a more straightforward skill that anyone can learn. Once we learn to be more responsible, we choose to take care of our own messes, including our impulses. If we are responsible, we behave ethically and kindly toward others, while always accepting responsibility for ourselves and our thoughts. If we are responsible, we don't blame others for our thoughts and emotions, and in heaven that's important, because our thoughts have a much more immediate response in the environment around us. And on those others in the afterlife. It makes sense to say that treating everyone with respect and acting more responsibly toward ourselves and others is a form of love.

In the special school, people who were irresponsible on earth and therefore harmed others are gently, lovingly, taught what responsibility is and why it's important, and are given the chance to work through things they experienced or did while in their physical bodies. In this way, they come to understand themselves. They now have enough information that they can decide to be better souls. They can take all the time they want to work through their lessons. They can take breaks from this inner work if they wish. The one restriction is that they can't leave the school until they learn to be sufficiently responsible that they no longer blame or harm others; instead, they must come to accept full responsibility for themselves and their choices, and learn to be better enough that they no longer choose to harm others.

But they aren't in any way forced, nor are they presented with boring lessons with no relationship to their reality and history. Instead, these folks are taught how to examine themselves so they can become more whole.

My opinion? We should all be taught how to be self-examining, self-correcting human beings while in physical reality. I'm not the first to say this and I won't be the last. Carl Jung advocated self-examination so we can all fully integrate and actualize ourselves. Abraham Maslow did likewise. Many other teachers, philosophers, and thinkers have suggested the same—that we all learn more responsible ways to think.

## *The nature of the afterlife requires responsibility*

The lessons taught in the special school are important because of the nature of the afterlife. Even though the afterlife looks like a physical place, it's not. It's made of pure energy, and is much more immediately responsive to our thoughts and intentions than the physical plane is. Imagine you are in heaven and you grow angry with someone (yes, that's possible in the afterlife—all emotions are valid) and you also aren't responsible enough with your energy. You might suddenly blast the person you're angry at with your energy, just as you did in life, but in heaven, the harm you do is immediately felt by the other. Or would be, if you were allowed to do that kind of thing. *No bueno*. (That means "no good" in Spanish.)

I've been asked by clients to communicate with certain people. When I contacted those folks, I found them in the special school. In the late 1980s, when I first started doing psychic readings, one soul I contacted was someone's grandfather who had done something horrible to my client; I caught a glimpse of some of what he'd done and I didn't want (or need) to see any more. He was in the special school and still had a lot of learning to do. At my request for communication, he was allowed to talk with me, and therefore pass along messages to my client, under careful supervision. He was allowed only a short communication in which he went through the motions of an apology, but it was much the sort of apology that's given through gritted teeth: the right words, but with no comprehension of why he needed to apologize and therefore no remorse. At the time I didn't know about the special school; I only knew that he was being kept somewhere I had never seen until then, and that place was separate from, but inside, heaven.

So the less responsible souls are kept separate until they learn self-control; and not just self-control. They learn why self-control and responsibility are important and why they need to treat everyone, regardless of how they feel about those people, with respect. As I said, no one is required to love or even like everyone—that's an impossible and unnecessary task. Yet everyone can and eventually must learn to be responsible for themselves, for their actions, and for how they treat others, and they can learn to treat everyone with respect, even those they don't agree with.

Souls in this special school are never forced or coerced or given a deadline. They learn at their own pace. When they are sent to this school, if they are quick learners, or are eager to become better beings, they might only spend a short time in the school. If they weren't and aren't any of those things, they stay longer. They can even refuse to learn at all, though they can't continue evolving and growing until they decide they want to learn what the special school teaches. Again, this special school is a loving, welcoming, respectful place and nobody is forced to do anything.

### *My mother contacted me after her death*

After her life review, which took about six months, my mother was sent to the special school in 2003, and she's still there. She's slowly learning to be a better being. Over the years, she's tried to communicate with me, and it's been educational to see her progress.

In the afterlife, where lies and denial are impossible, she remembers everything, but still has all the justifications and "reasons" for her behavior that she had in physical life. One of her justifications was that she had no choice but to abuse me because she was abused in her childhood. She's gradually coming to understand that she did have choices and that she made choices that were harmful to others. She's learning why she made those choices and what the consequences of the harm she did have been for herself and others. Over the years, she's tried to apologize to me, but her apologies were empty because she didn't understand how she'd done any harm; she was still justifying her actions by blaming everyone else. In her final contact with me, she didn't try to apologize, because she still didn't understand the harm she's done, but at least she'd come to recognize that she did harm. Having learned enough responsibility to respect my desire for no contact, she hasn't tried to contact me again.

She's now chosen to start the inner work she avoided when in a body. It's too late to help me or any of the other people she harmed while she was on earth, but not too late for her. She's starting to accept more responsibility for her choices and actions. And because she's learned enough, she now understands why it's not a good idea to try to override anyone's free will. Since I had told her that I wasn't interested in further communication with her, she is being responsible and has stopped trying to communicate with me. She never loved me in life and as far as I can tell, she doesn't love me in her afterlife either. (When she was in a body, she went through impressive verbal gymnastics to avoid saying "I love you" to me, such as saying "You are loved" rather than "I love you." And I can count on one hand how many times she used even that phrase toward me.) The only warmth she and I shared when she was on earth was a mutual enjoyment of some earthly things, such as movies and cooking.

It's good to hear that she's making headway in her healing. I want her to be whole and happy, and it sounds like she's getting there. Yet although I'm glad she's finally getting her act together, we have nothing to say to each other as souls.

The message here is that it's never too late for any soul, even the most demonic, to choose to turn to the good.

## *How do you graduate from the special school? What happens then?*

To graduate from the special school, you need to have accepted responsibility for yourself and to have learned how to be responsible. There's no way to cheat your teachers or pull the wool over their eyes or in any way be released until you well and truly learn these core lessons. Once you've done that, you're released into the general grounds of heaven.

## *Not everyone goes through their life review right away*

After my experience of dropping in on my mother in her life review, and after talking with enough people in the afterlife after their life reviews, I came to accept that the life review was real. I used to think it was the first thing we do when we reach the afterlife, and that everyone had to go through it immediately upon reaching the afterlife.

However, I now know that not everyone immediately goes through a life review.

I found this out when doing some ancestral work in late 2023. I discovered that neither my paternal grandfather nor his father, my paternal great-grandfather, have gone through their life reviews. I psychically saw them both with their arms crossed and heads down, chins on their chests, eyes not shut but also not looking at anything. They know they did a great deal of harm in life, yet even now mulishly refuse to accept responsibility for the harm they did in the faint hope that if they never admit it, it didn't happen.

They don't want to do their life reviews because they know they're going to have to admit they harmed others, and when they did that harm, they often hurt those others quite badly.

Meanwhile, until they're ready, they sit in the special school. They aren't exactly stuck, but they sure aren't moving forward.

When I asked for information on why they're like that, I received the answer that they both felt betrayed by a woman they initially perceived as friendly, but whom they later came to view as Eve, tempting them to evil. They blame these women, whom I believe may represent their wives, for their own bad actions. The women they blame are also something of an archetype for them in an "all women are Eve" way of thinking, where Eve is the only person at fault in the story of the Garden of Eden. "She made me do it!" is not a good look.

Paradoxically, in a masterful display of mental gymnastics, my paternal grandfather and great-grandfather are simultaneously blaming someone else for their harmful actions, and denying they ever did anything harmful. They don't yet see that they can't both say someone else made them do harmful things and deny they've ever done harmful things.

To move on in the afterlife, my paternal grandfather and great-grandfather must first stop blaming others, accept accountability, and let go of their preconceptions and misconceptions. You can't deal with a problem until you acknowledge it. But for now they're setting a record for how long a soul can stubbornly refuse to admit anything.

They're sitting in their own self-generated cloud of denial in the special school, separated from others so they can no longer harm anyone. They're quite content to sit in the dumpster fire of their denials, pretending they're fine, everything is fine, they never harmed anyone, any harm they might have done was at someone else's instigation and therefore not their fault, and there are no consequences to anything they've done.

My paternal grandparent and paternal great-grandparent will be in the special school until they decide to go through their life reviews and then start to learn to be better beings. No rush. Nobody's going to make them do anything. Turns out free will extends even to your choice of when to do your life review. You *must* do it eventually, when you decide (if you decide) you want to continue to evolve and grow as a soul, but you get to choose *when* you do it. Maybe when everyone else has left you behind, you might start to get some FOMO (fear of missing out) and then start your inner work.

It can be reassuring to some people to know that the pace they take for doing their inner work, for learning more about themselves and others, for becoming better souls, is completely up to them. Especially if a person lived in coercive circumstances during their life on earth, it can be a relief to know that once you arrive in the afterlife, nobody will force you to do anything ever again.

## *Is there life after the afterlife?*

Is there life after the afterlife? Yes.

If we want, we can move on from heaven. As souls that exist multidimensionally, we can continue to evolve and explore and grow. As the god Loki once told me, "Even gods evolve." Most gods and goddesses didn't start as gods or goddesses—they evolved their way there.

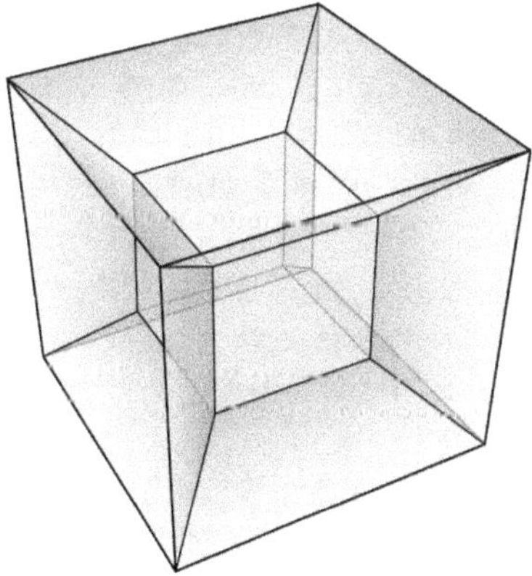

*Figure 9. A tesseract—a representation of four dimensions as seen in three dimensions—is a good analogy for our existence after heaven.*

Just as we human beings don't have to evolve spiritually while in a physical body, we also don't have to evolve in the afterlife. We can stay at whatever level we want. But why would we want to stay there? To me, that's stagnation. Sometimes we need to take a break from growing, but the break shouldn't last forever. Though that's my opinion arising out of my desire to always work on becoming a better being. Maybe I just don't know enough about the grand scheme of things to know that it's okay to never want to move forward from where you are.

Souls in heaven are still alive, and they're on their own unique path. They continue to evolve and grow in different ways. Many souls stay in heaven because they're working on the various projects I mentioned a few chapters ago, and they're working on themselves. They're having a great time, and they can stay as long as they want. Eventually some of them evolve enough that they don't want to stay in heaven; they want to move on to their next great adventure.

If, after working on your various fun heavenly projects, you want to move on to other dimensions and see what more there is to life, you can.

I've only sometimes, and unclearly at that, glimpsed what's beyond heaven. The closest analogy I can come up with is that our reality as multidimensional beings is like a grid of an infinite number of intersecting lines of energy going up and down and back and forth across each other throughout time and space (a good representation of how this looks to me is shown in figure 5 in chapter 2). Each of us exists along all those lines and can access our existences at any of the points on those lines.

The intersections are where versions of ourselves are energetically closer to other versions, meaning we can more easily communicate through time and space with those other selves at those points. In the 2014 movie, *Interstellar*, the tesseract (a four-dimensional construct) is similar to how I imagine our multidimensional existence looks like.

We can communicate with other selves throughout time and space, but we don't always need to; much of the time such communications would be like exchanging cross-dimensional chit-chat. "How are you today? How are the cats?" sort of thing. Sometimes, though, we have something useful to say to each other. Not that chit-chat isn't useful, but can you imagine how overwhelming it would be to get constant communications on everything from all our existences throughout time and space and beyond? Although we can and do get that communication, most of the time we ignore it while living in physical reality.

It's easier for our related selves in our various physical-reality lives to communicate with related versions of ourselves (by related selves, I mean incarnated souls who are from the same greater soul; for more on this idea, see chapter 8, which is on reincarnation) in physical-reality lives when we are at the same age, or when we are undergoing similar experiences.

For example, let's say you're 30 years old, and you're facing a difficult decision. Suddenly you start receiving information relevant to that decision. Or you start experiencing a success in your personal expression that you feel another self is also experiencing elsewhere in time and space. It could be the received information is from spiritual helpers, or it could be the information is from a related soul who is also 30 years old in another time and place, or who is experiencing the same kind of success. That kind of information is always available, but we are more open to receiving it at certain times in our lives.

We all continue to evolve and grow—each soul a part of its greater soul, exploring reality, learning, experimenting, and sharing what's learned with our related souls and with our greater soul.

Sometimes when I speak with highly evolved entities, they use the pronoun "we" instead of "I." This isn't the royal "we." Instead, they are speaking from the totality of their existence—all their related souls—as they have evolved. They are speaking from their greater soul's perspective. We each will get to that point where we do the same—our individual awarenesses merge back into our greater soul's awareness, and yet we are also aware of our individual souls.

And one final thought for this chapter: The mysterious and unseen are everywhere, both in physical reality and in the nonphysical world. It's not this book's topic, but beings like fairies—the Fae—exist (and are canonically recognized as real by the Catholic church; Saint Augustine wrote about them and said the Fae had never fallen, which is one reason we humans don't understand them). In my experiences as a psychic, I've spoken with many kinds of folks, human and nonhuman, and won't rule out the existence of others I haven't yet encountered. Reality is wide, amazing, and complex.

# Chapter 4
# Everyone and everything has free will

Free will means being able to decide and act without interference or coercion from the Divine, destiny, fate, or something similar. People have debated whether we have free will for millennia.

What do you believe about free will? Do you believe we have the freedom to choose? Do you think that someone or something divine makes choices for you? Do you believe, as the American psychologist B. F. Skinner did, that there is no such thing as free will, and that instead all that we think and feel arises from our physical existence, and that our actions are the result of previous actions and outside influence from our environment?

You can reduce the argument about free will to two camps: we have it, or we don't. All other discussions are variations of the two camps.

In favor of us having free will, the argument is that a Divine creator would love us enough to give us free will, and that any decisions we made if we didn't have free will would have no value or meaning. What do I mean by "no value or meaning"? I mean that if we are coerced to do something, that action isn't our choice and is meaningless in terms of our character as a human being. If we aren't forced to do anything, but instead can freely make choices, then our choices made out of our free will are immensely important.

In favor of not having free will, the arguments are that we're subject to fate—things happen beyond our control; we're subject to destiny—certain things are meant to happen to us, and there's nothing we can do to change that, though there's a layer of "you're destined for great things; we're subject to predestination —all events are willed by God, God makes everything happen, we have no choice in making any actions, and so on.

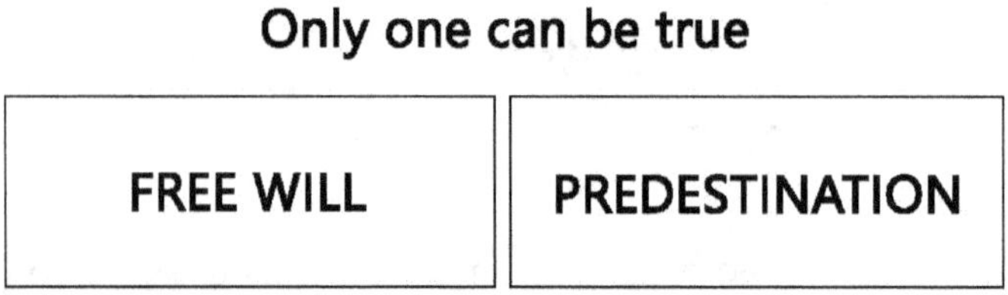

**Only one can be true**

| FREE WILL | PREDESTINATION |
|---|---|

*Figure 10. Either we have free will or we don't.*

I believe we all have free will down to the bare metal of the universe. It's a gift and a condition of our existence. I agree with many others that it wouldn't make sense for a Divine creator to give us a soupçon of free will, only to yank away the value of our choices by imposing events on us beyond our choice. Even if the Divine desires us all to choose the good, there would be no meaning to that choice if we were all marionettes manipulated by the Divine or other forces to do what those forces want us to, to be controlled into doing either good or evil actions.

This gets into touchy territory. Many people blame God for every bad thing that happens (and also praise God for every good thing). "God made that harmful event happen, so it must be God's will that we suffered." Or, after a successful medical procedure, "Thank God the procedure was a success!" But what about the physicians who performed that procedure? Did they not have anything to do with the success? "Oh, well, God made the physician do it right."

I disagree with the "God made me do it" arguments. They're all ways to avoid responsibility, and reveal a deep fear and hatred of the Divine. I prefer not to think of us all as nothing more than God's puppets. What kind of loving creators would give the gift of life and not also include the gift of free will? What meaning would be in anything we do if we are being shoved around on the chessboard of life? What meaning are acts of kindness, then? Or, for that matter, what meaning are acts of cruelty, if some Divine being made us do it?

We all make choices, whether we're fully conscious of them or not. Our choices affect the world for good or ill. Though we may sometimes wish we could, we can't avoid responsibility for those choices, or ignore the effects our choices have on ourselves and others. For more on how effective our thinking is on both ourselves and others, see Dawson Church's *Mind to Matter:*

*The Astonishing Science of How Your Brain Creates Material Reality* (Hay House Inc., 2018).

## *Angels have free will, and so do we*

Angels exist, so many that they are uncountable by normal means. I see angels as divine beings who help physical and spiritual reality. I see individual angels, whom I call guardian angels, tending every client I've had. I also see angels tending everything in reality, from the tiniest atom to entire planets, solar systems, galaxies, and beyond, with Metatron, who, as I said in an earlier chapter, is often called the voice for God, in charge of all of physical reality and the multivers. In that sense there's an angelic hierarchy, but no one angel's tasks are more important than another.

*Figure 11. Angels have areas of responsibility, from an atom to the multiverse.*

"Multiverse" refers to the idea that reality comprises more than one universe, including many dimensions, and that possibly we even each have alternate selves existing in other universes and dimensions.

For decades, some folks in the New Age crowd have been passing around the belief that angels don't have free will. My understanding is different. Of course angels have free will. Why would the Divine give everyone free will except some of the highest and most holy beings?

I think the misunderstanding comes from people seeing that angels make the best choices. Those people then interpret that as meaning that angels can make no other choice and therefore angels have no free will.

But that mistaken idea shows a profound misunderstanding of free will. The more dedicated you are to doing the right thing in all situations, and the more aware you are of what the right thing is, the more you choose to do the right thing. Just as no one forces you to make wrong choices, no one forces you to make the right ones. Choosing the right thing because to you that's the only right choice might look like a lack of choice to onlookers, but it's not. Ursula Le Guin said something similar in her book, *A Wizard of Earthsea* (Parnassus Press, 1968): "as a man's real power grows and his knowledge widens, ever the way he can follow grows narrower: until at last he chooses nothing, but does only and wholly what he *must* do."

It's a matter of responsibility. The more responsible you are, the more you choose to accept responsibility for your actions rather than blame someone else for your choices, and the more you choose to do the right thing even if it's difficult. In fact, if you are that evolved, it becomes nearly impossible to do the wrong thing. You simply can't make that choice.

We've all heard, "It's their fault! They made me do it! I wouldn't have done those things if it weren't for them! They made me so angry I couldn't help myself!"

No. Nobody can make someone else feel emotions such as anger, or sadness, or happiness. No one has that much power over anyone else, not even the Divine. No one can force us to feel or do anything we don't want to.

You might be asking, "But what if someone is beating us or threatening our lives? Aren't they making us feel frightened or angry?"

No. We choose what we want to feel and how to respond. It can be hard, sometimes quite, quite hard, to make the right choice, but it's imperative for the sake of us as souls inhabiting a human body. In their book, *Made for Goodness: And Why This Makes All the Difference* (HarperOne, 2010), Desmond Tutu and his daughter Mpho Tutu tell the story of Phila Portia Ndwandwe, a woman who was kidnapped, beaten, and probably raped. Her captors were trying to get her to betray a group she belonged to. If she had, many more people would have been beaten and worse.

Despite her horrific treatment, Phila never gave the information. When she didn't break, she was murdered. Did she know she was going to die? Almost certainly. Did she use that knowledge as an excuse to give up her principles? No.

As the Tutus say about Phila, she knew that "opting for the easy wrong may save the body, but it kills the soul."

We as souls are immortal, but opting for the easy wrong diminishes us and those around us, and in that way we are damaging ourselves. As Socrates said, we all know right and wrong, which means we all know when we are doing the right or wrong thing. When we choose to do the wrong thing, we're harming ourselves or others, and we tarnish our opinion of ourselves and the opinion others have of us. And one bad act makes the next bad act easier. Each time we choose to do bad things, we move further away from our center, from our true nature, from all that is good, from the divine inside us. We're taking a thorny path that becomes increasingly more difficult to move away from.

Eventually, in this life or at some point in our existence past this life, if we've been walking a dark path, we might decide to start walking back toward the light of goodness. But just as we traveled that thorny path one choice at a time, we must also work our way back one choice at a time. Despite what you see in movies, bad people don't suddenly become good people. They *can* become better, but it's not instant. It takes time and work and responsibility and sometimes backsliding and sometimes giving up entirely for a while until we regain our desire to walk the hard road back to ourselves. But the further we walk ourselves back down the road to goodness, the easier it gets.

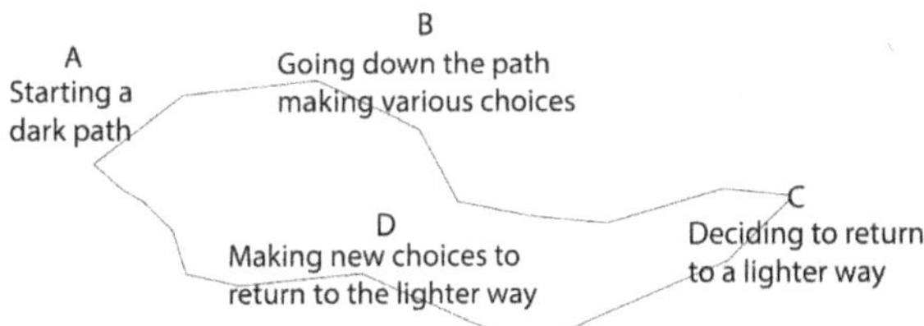


*Figure 12. Even if we've walked down dark paths, even if we've gone a long way down that path, the distance doesn't matter. We can still choose to walk back toward the Divine.*

On the other hand, opting for the difficult right action burnishes the soul, and makes the next good act easier. I am sure that after Phila's bodily death, she took with her the choices she'd made to save other people's lives. And with her, all other choices she made while on this earth. The choices that helped make her a better human being also enriched her as a soul.

I hope you are never faced with the choice between your life and your soul. More likely, you, as are we all, are faced with daily small occurrences with their attendant choices. You may have the choice of lying or telling the truth about something. You may think that if you lie, you won't have to face someone's displeasure. If you tell the truth, you face someone's response, a response you would rather avoid—their anger or disappointment or sadness or rejection or some other uncomfortable response. In such a case, lying is the easy wrong.

If we opt for the easy wrong, we avoid those consequences for now, except our private regrets and a diminished sense of self. Yet we can learn from making poor choices. We can think about what we did, and can choose to learn about ourselves—why we made that choice, how we could have chosen differently—and we can choose to act differently the next time.

We don't have to choose to learn from our mistakes while in a physical body. In the afterlife, we review every choice we made while alive here on earth, and we can learn from our choices then. But once in the afterlife, we can't do much to help those we harmed. If in physical life we harm people through bad choices, and never change our actions or make amends for the wrongs we're doing, we can't fix it in the afterlife. At the most, once we are in the afterlife, we can ask for Divine help for the people we harmed, and can send the people we harmed messages of hope and regret. (Assuming we care about them, which is debatable because, if we cared about them, we would never have hurt them repeatedly in life.)

Just as the good we do lives on after us, the harm we do lives on long after our death. This is where we get generational trauma, where parents pass their trauma on to their children, and those children pass on their trauma to their children, on and on until someone in some generation stops the cycle. (Which can and does happen.)

So why wait? Why not start now, while we're able to do something about our choices? Why not start doing the hard work of taking responsibility for ourselves now? Why not start learning to be better human beings now?

If you are in a bad situation, your choice is to get out of that situation as quickly and as safely as you can. If you're experiencing domestic violence, most countries have agencies to help people in your situation. If you're experiencing a terrorist situation, do as Phila did and stay true to your principles. Yes, your bodily life matters, but you as a soul matter more.

## *We choose everything down to the bare metal of the universe*

Because we all have free will, we make *all* our decisions consciously. Yet as Seth (a spirit who gave messages through a woman named Jane Roberts) said, as soon as we make many of our decisions of what we want to experience, we instantly bury the awareness and memory of our decision so that life comes as a continuous surprise to us. Then we ask ourselves, "Where did that come from? Why did that happen?"

I've caught myself making that kind of decision a few times. In one case it was about the kind of traffic flow I wanted to experience as I pulled out onto a busy street from my quiet neighborhood. I felt myself making the decision, felt a kind of reaching out as the traffic flow adjusted itself to my decision, then felt the decision try to flee from my conscious thoughts and memory. It leaves quite an impression to see how everything, including traffic flow, is subject to free will.

But most of us, including me, hide this deep kind of "constructing our reality" awareness from ourselves most of the time.

As an instructor at Santa Clara University once told me, most of us walk around deeply asleep, unconscious and unaware of ourselves or others. I didn't know what he meant at the time; I've since observed that truth for myself. Most people aren't aware of the choices they make in daily life, let alone foresee or understand the consequences of their choices; they are asleep, as that instructor said, and aren't self-aware. Researchers have found that, "although 95% of people think they're self-aware, only 10 to 15% actually are." (Source: "Working with People Who Aren't Self-Aware," by Tasha Eurich. https://hbr.org/2018/10/working-with-people-who-arent-self-aware, October 19, 2018; retrieved September 8, 2024.)

The takeaway here is that you might believe things happen to you, but it could be you're doing things, making choices, that lead to certain outcomes. Becoming more self-aware can help you learn about yourself so you can change any trends you don't like. It can be liberating to understand that you have free will and aren't subject to outside manipulation. Or, if you prefer to play the victim, it can be frightening to think that only you are responsible for your state. I talk more about how to become more self-aware and responsible in chapter 12.

# Chapter 5
# How the dead communicate with us

Often, people who have left their bodies and are now in heaven want to talk with us. Because of free will (discussed in chapter 4), the dearly departed can't *make* us do anything; the most they can do is give us strong suggestions on what they think is right for us. In many cases, they now have a wider perspective and more information to base their suggestions on. (See chapter 14 for one example of this kind of greater awareness.) But not always. Sometimes they are unaware of what's best for us. And because they aren't always right about what's right for us, and because it's never good to give up our agency to anyone else, it's still up to us to weigh what they say against common sense and our internal sense of rightness. (If you aren't familiar with the word "agency," it means being in control of your life, making your own decisions to further yourself on your path. The opposite of having agency is feeling like and acting as though you are a victim of circumstances and other people.)

The same is true for any communications we receive from anyone and any being in the spirit realm, not just the dearly departed: Other beings can suggest, but we get to decide whether to listen. Making that judgment call is important especially when we are just learning to be open to spirit communications, because some spirits don't have our best interests in mind and will try to lead us astray. Some souls can make themselves look and sound good—saying all the right words—but if you're alert, you might notice they don't *feel* right. Those are deceivers. Deceivers often play on your fears or your ego, trying to make you feel important. I've sometimes heard clients say that "I'm special because entity X—who is a big deal in the spiritual realm—talks with me!" Yet when I check in with that entity, they aren't who they say; they're just preying on an innocent person. When such show up and you realize they are deceivers, ask for Divine help in having them removed from your presence. Better yet, ask for Divine help in preventing any such from coming close to you. If asking for help doesn't give you the needed relief, consult with an ethical, competent psychic.

Sometimes people give up their agency by saying they were compelled by a spirit to do something. That way, if any negative consequences happen, they can deny responsibility by blaming their choices on the spirit. One theme threaded throughout this book is that responsibility is a more evolved approach than victimhood and blame. Be wary of folks who don't accept responsibility for their choices and actions.

If the dearly departed do have our best interests in mind, and do have something useful to say, they can communicate with us in many ways. That doesn't mean we get the message. Sometimes we aren't open to the possibility of receiving such messages, or sometimes, even if we are, we don't know how to receive or even recognize those messages. We are often most open to receiving those messages in the dream state, though the more energetically sensitive of us can also receive and recognize them while awake. And the dearly departed can also send us messages in other ways, as I discuss later.

If you're used to thinking of dreams as internal, private things that have nothing to do with anything, consider an alternative notion: Dreams aren't just one thing only. It's true that sometimes a dream may be just "an undigested bit of beef," as Ebenezer Scrooge says to the ghost of Jacob Marley in Charles Dickens's *A Christmas Carol* (Chapman & Hall, 1843). That is, the dream could simply be our bodies processing something we ate.

Yet also many times in our dreams we are working on our internal psychological landscape and working through short- or long-term problems. And frequently in our dreams we are romping about in the greater reality of the universe beyond the physical, interacting with others who are likewise exploring. And sometimes those others we meet when dreaming are people who are no longer in the physical world; that is, they are the dearly (or not so dearly) departed. In those cases, we can converse with them and receive their messages more easily than when waking.

A note of caution: If you are having a lucid dream—meaning a dream in which you are in your mostly normal conscious state, aware that you are dreaming—it's super important to not try to change or control things. That's because you are interacting with other living beings, not with internal dream images. If you try to change the dream, you are trying to override the free will of those others you are sharing the dream with. Such an effort is instantly shut down, and the person trying to change things is moved to a safe playground where they *think* they're controlling the energetic landscape and other people, but are in fact just messing around with the Play-Doh of reality rather than with other living beings.

In my experiences of recording and studying my own dreams starting when I was 13, and reading about dreams throughout the decades, I've come to believe that our dreams bring messages to us from a number of sources, including our greater selves, that is, the selves we are outside space and time; other people or spirits who wish to communicate with us for good or ill; and, as is relevant to this book, the dearly departed—people who are no longer with us. The dearly departed could be ancestors; it could be people who were close to us but who have now moved away from this earth; and it could be beings who, for whatever reason, want to get a message to us. We are most open to such messages when we're asleep.

Yes, I'm saying we all can talk with the dead in our dreams, assuming the departed want to talk with us. And many of them most definitely do want to talk with us, especially if we think of them often. If we're grieving, they'd like us to know that they are fine and that we will see them again when it's our turn to leave the earthly plane. That reassurance doesn't take away the grief—we still miss them and wish they were here in the physical world with us. Knowing someone's soul still lives isn't nearly as cozy and companionable as sharing a cup of tea and some scones with them in physical reality. But it can assuage any fears we have that they are suffering some kind of punishment, or worse yet, have been obliterated and are no longer anywhere.

Our spirit friends find it easiest, sometimes, to communicate with us in our dreams because although they aren't constrained by time and space, we who are still in human bodies are constrained by our beliefs. Waking, we find all manner of reasons to dismiss and ignore communications that are out of the ordinary because many of us don't believe in invisible things. Yet an invisible world exists in and around the physical world we see. Asleep, we tend to relax such defenses against the unseen, and so our dearly departed can more easily tell us what they want us to hear.

## *Symbols, communication, and meaning*

In the realms of spirit and energy, existence looks quite different from physical reality. Therefore, communication and meanings are conveyed through symbols. A symbol is a compact image that contains meaning. For example, in figure 13 are some symbols for our sun. Some are universal: a circle with some kind of rays surrounding it is a simple images representing the sun. One image, the circle with the dot inside, is the alchemical and astrological symbol for the sun. Each image is a symbol that carries with it the meanings of life, warmth, and all other associations we have with the sun. When someone looks at one of these symbols, they consciously or unconsciously "read" the image (symbol) as both a representation of the sun, and also all the other meanings the sun symbol carries.

*Figure 13. Three symbols representing the sun. Though different, each symbol is understood as meaning the sun.*

The same is true for all symbols. They are images that represent something—either a physical thing or a concept. People in the culture that uses those symbols understand their meanings. Symbols therefore carry a great deal of semantic content and are shortcuts for ideas. Because they are richly meaningful, symbols can be shared across many cultures and can last through centuries, even millennia.

Two examples of symbols that carry such a rich load of meaning that they have lasted for centuries are runes and tarot cards. Runes are a writing system that goes back millennia. They are also symbols that contain within them gateways to the totality of existence, both physical and nonphysical. (Two nonphysical entities gave me this information.) Tarot cards, which normally come in a deck of 78 cards, are each filled with symbols that have a multitude of meanings, and each card also corresponds to a human archetype. By "archetype," I mean a collection of meaningful, universal traits that apply to specific types of human behavior. For example, the devouring mother who destroys her children is an archetype, and so is the wise person, or the innocent person. We each embody one or more archetypes, and those archetypes can change as we change, or can vary depending on our circumstances. A devouring mother may be harming her child or children, but might express the saint archetype to other people.

We humans use symbols in everyday life; for example, traffic signs often symbols, and we use symbols that are recognized internationally for many everyday things. All languages use symbols, such as letters, sounds, or ideograms, that can be combined to make words with meaning. Artists use symbols, either blatantly or subtly, to convey meaning in their work. If you're interested, you can find many resources on symbols—books, websites, and other such media. Just be aware that some people make things up. If they don't cite their sources, do your own research. Otherwise you have no way of knowing whether what an author says is credible or just ego-inspired porky pies. ("Porky pie" is Cockney rhyming slang meaning "lies.")

## *Symbols and dreams*

Symbols are the main form through which communications from the greater reality are conveyed. When we dream, we experience portions of that greater reality. When we wake, our minds translate the reality of what we experienced into symbols that we can understand in terms we recognize from our physical reality. Our memories of our dreams are symbolic reconstructions of what we experienced. What we remember from our time spent in the greater reality when dreaming is quite often a translation of our dream experiences into symbols that mean something to us in this life. If this interests you and you want to learn more about your dreams and your dream symbols, it's useful to keep a record of your dreams. Try to figure out what they mean.

After a while, you start to learn your own symbols—what it means when you dream of a specific action or image.

If we dream of swimming, when we wake, we can gain insight into ourselves by thinking about and asking ourselves questions about the dream. What kind of water were we swimming in? A pond, a lake, a swimming pool, the ocean? How did we feel while swimming? Were we comfortable, uneasy, frightened, overwhelmed? Were we alone, or were others present? If alone, how did that feel? If others were present, how did we feel around them? And so on. In asking these questions, we can start to understand a great deal about ourselves, both in the long run and in our daily lives.

One note: Many people have written books on dream symbols. Most of those books are only a starting point. There are seldom any symbols that mean the same thing to everyone. If you're drawn to such books, by all means explore! But be a trifle skeptical, and be open to learning your individual dream symbol meanings.

## *An example of learning your dream symbols*

Throughout my life, I often dreamed of fish, sometimes lovely fish in a home aquarium, sometimes larger fish in a swimming pool, sometimes fish in the wild. After many such dreams, I came to understand that in my dream symbology, fish represent thoughts and ideas. I came to this understanding through writing about the dreams and what I thought they meant as related to my everyday life, and through correlating my dreams with events.

*Figure 14. Learning your dream symbols can be fun.*

While writing this book, I dreamed I was using large, tightly woven baskets to catch substantially sized fish falling from the sky. In the dream, I knew I was going to share the fish as food with many people. When I woke, pairing my personal dream meaning of fish with the act of writing this book, the dream's meaning was clear: I'm sharing my ideas with everyone who reads this book, and it's my hope that my ideas are nourishing. I don't expect everyone to find value in everything I write, but if even a handful of people are better prepared for the afterlife because they read my book, then I've been of service.

The takeaway is that your dreams are important and, if you pay attention to them, can reveal truths to you about yourself and others.

## *Sometimes dreams tell of coming events*

Although many dreams are messages meant only for us, sometimes we're told of coming events. Whether we can do anything about those events is another matter.

In the week preceding March 11, 2011, I dreamed repeatedly of a tsunami inundating a city somewhere far west of me. (I live on the West Coast of the United States, and there aren't any close cities west of me; there's just the Pacific Ocean.) I thought perhaps the dreams were symbolic, but I had no clue what they meant. I thought if the dream wasn't symbolic, then it was possible a tsunami was going to happen, but I saw nothing specific in the dreams that told me when or where the tsunami would happen. You may remember that Japan was hit by a devastating tsunami on March 11, 2011. After the fact, I was sure I'd been warned of the tsunami, but without anything substantial anchoring the dream images to a place, I had no way of doing anything about the warning.

Other times, I've dreamed something trivial would happen, and it would indeed happen as I dreamed. That kind of dream seems useless, though I'm sure there's a reason for them.

I caution you not to think that every dream you have is about something that's about to happen. If you don't practice judgment, discernment, and common sense, you can get yourself worked up over nothing. I've heard anecdotal stories of people dreaming their partners were cheating on them, then accusing their partner when they woke. What the dreams could have meant was the dreamer was feeling insecure, or was picking up that their partner, though not cheating, wasn't committed to the relationship. It's irresponsible to accuse someone of doing something you dreamed they did. That kind of reaction is why I recommend you pay attention to your dreams and learn the meanings of your dream language symbols. Always ask yourself what the dream might mean aside from representing coming or actual events. You'll learn more about yourself that way.

## *Dreams carry messages from the spirit realm*

As I said earlier, many truths of the spirit realm are communicated through symbols. When we dream, we are often in a greater reality whose appearance and substance is quite different from physical reality. When we wake, our minds translate what we experienced in our dreams into symbols and images that can make sense to us. What we experienced when dreaming looked nothing like what we remember when we wake. The dream images we remember are translations from that greater reality into physical-reality symbols that we can understand. If you're interested in expanding your ability to communicate with other beings, it helps to pay attention to and think about your dreams and the symbols in them.

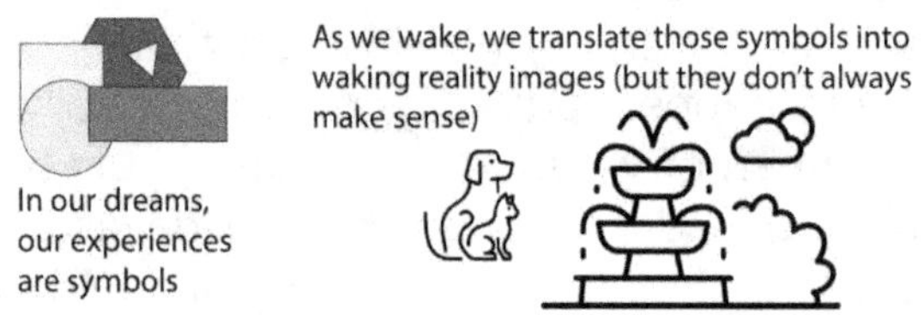


*Figure 15. When we dream, we're in a greater reality whose images and symbols differ from waking reality. Once we wake, we translate what we experienced into symbols and images that make sense in our physical world.*

If, for example, you dream of your beloved grandmother, that could mean she is trying to give you a message, *or* it could mean whatever your grandmother meant to you. If she was a kind, loving, giving person, dreaming of her might be a reminder to you to be more like grandma, or a reminder that someone loved you, or it could mean something else. The more familiar you are with your dream symbols, the easier it will be for you to figure out what a specific dream of your grandmother (or anything and anyone else) means.

If it was your grandmother communicating with you through your dream (and many of our dearly departed do communicate with us that way), and if your grandmother was a loving person whom you also loved, then pay attention to the message. You might not agree with her, but it could be that she has something valuable to tell you that she sees from her wider perspective in the afterlife.

## *An example message from a dearly departed*

While writing this book, I dreamed I visited a family friend who died long ago. She had a Buddhism-like set of beliefs. When I visited her in the dream, she was in an empty world. She showed me around where she was living, which, when I woke, my mind translated as a version of Berkeley, California, a city in and around which she spent most of her life. But there was no one else there. She was still the same person I'd known my entire life, and she didn't seem to care that she was alone. When I woke, I speculated that for now, she's in an empty world because she expected emptiness after death. And maybe what I saw as an empty city, she might have been seeing as a completely different place, yet still empty. Eventually she may realize that she doesn't have to be alone, but for now she's content. The message I drew from this dream was that it could be useful to share my experiences of feeling one with everything.

Some people talk about oneness with everything as though it means the dissolution of our being into a great nothingness, and that dissolution is an ideal to be sought. Or that we meld into a vast sea of consciousness and lose awareness of ourselves. Someone once told me he believes we're all interchangeable energy components and that when we die, we're fragmented into unaware energy pieces, like a pack of batteries, and our energy is reused to construct new awarenesses. This belief is a kind of collage approach to creation.

I've experienced oneness with everything a few times, and it has never been nothingness or a loss of myself. Instead, it is an awareness of and connection with everything. When I experienced oneness, I was still aware of myself as an individual, and I also felt the presence of everything around me, and knew what those other beings were feeling.

In one instance of feeling oneness, I was driving home north on Interstate 10 from where I worked south of Tucson, Arizona. Without transition, I was suddenly in communication with all beings for miles around—the birds perched on a telephone wire, the coyotes moving purposefully through the plants in the high desert (saguaros and various other cactuses, ocotillos, creosote bush, and the many other plants native to the Sonoran High Desert), the plants themselves, and all other living things in the area. Far from being dissolved in nothingness, I joined everything else in the joy of being alive. I could move my attention from one being to another—bird, coyote, snake, and so on—and feel their acknowledgment of my existence just as I acknowledged theirs. This sense of oneness in no way interfered with my ability to drive my car and be aware of my surroundings. If anything, it enhanced my ability to drive safely because of my being in tune with everything.

I've felt this oneness a few times in my life. Each time, it's been peaceful and delightful. Having had these experiences, I sometimes wonder why people prefer the idea of oneness equating nothingness instead of the idea of oneness meaning a connection with all living things. Perhaps, for some people at least, the appeal of nothingness is two things: the release of any sense of responsibility, and the release of any fear of what reprisals one might suffer in the afterlife for one's misdeeds in this life. Often the idea that we shouldn't get attached to anything goes hand-in-glove with the view that dissolving into nothingness is ultimately desirable. For many, lack of attachment seems to mean not caring, but as I say in chapter 6, emotions are vital both here and in the afterlife. Caring for others is an emotion. What would be the point of life if we don't care about anything or anyone? My experience of oneness wasn't attachment, but it also wasn't an uncaring detachment. Maybe I just don't understand the idea of not being attached.

## *Other ways the dearly departed send us messages*

The dearly departed send us messages in other ways than dreams. Many truths and messages are communicated to us through synchronicity. Synchronicity means two or more seemingly unrelated things happening at the same time in such a way that we can gain meaning from those events; the events seem connected in a way without there being a cause for them to happen at the same time. Sometimes synchronicity can be as simple as hearing the same song in several ways: on the internet or radio, at someone's house, mentioned in a message to you, and so on.

Hearing a song once can be considered a happenstance; twice is starting to get your attention; three or more times and it's a message. It could be a message from the spirit realm, from the Divine, from another living being (human or otherwise), from your greater soul as it exists outside space and time, from your guardian angel, or possibly from a dearly departed person.

You might hear a song on the radio that meant something to your departed mother, or you might see something unusual that you associate with your departed father, or you might smell something you associate with a departed friend when the smell has no source, or you may see something in a book or on TV or in a movie that seems significant, and so on. All those could be random, or they could be messages. You get to decide.

Sometimes, if we're paying attention, we can become aware of small, gentle, almost imperceptible nudges from our intuition, telling us to say something, be somewhere, do something, or not do something. That guidance can come from the greater, more aware part of ourselves, from our greater self, from the dearly departed who love us, from ancestors (more on ancestors in chapter 10), and from angels and other divine guides. We often don't know why we're being guided, and sometimes we never figure it out, but once we've ascertained that it's genuine guidance, it's worthwhile to trust that guidance.

It's up to you to decide whether you want to receive these communications, and from whom. Just because someone wants to communicate with you, doesn't mean you must communicate with them. Just say "no" if you want to refuse the communication.

## *Communicating more formally with the dead*

In addition to what can be considered casual, unstructured communications through dreams and synchronicity, we can also communicate more formally with the dearly departed. One way to do so is to consult a reputable medium. A medium is a psychic who can communicate with people who have moved on. All mediums—the legit ones, anyway—are psychic, but not all psychics are mediums. That is, many psychics can't communicate with the departed, or don't want to.

If you want to consult a medium, be careful. A lot of people claim to be psychics who aren't and are only running scams on people. And some people have genuine psychic abilities but no ethics. I've encountered this latter sort a few times when meeting other psychics: They think that because they can get information about others psychically, that it's okay to pry and get that information. And then they use that information to manipulate others. The idea that just because they *can* do something doesn't mean they *should* do that something just never occurs to them. If you're consulting a psychic, ask them what their code of ethics is. If their code doesn't include "never without permission," find someone else. Also ask if they are keeping records on their clients—recordings of their readings, for example, or even a database of clients. I never do any of that—when clients want a recording, I make it available to them in a secure location for a month, then delete it forever. Nor do I keep a database of clients —that seems invasive and unnecessary.

If you're drawn to communicating with the dearly departed, you can work on developing your own abilities to send and receive messages. I can't tell you how to do that in this book, though I can give you some basics:

1. Be as self-aware as you can be.
2. Be honest with yourself and others.
3. Be kind, empathetic, and compassionate with yourself and others.
4. Have an open mind and be adaptable.

5. Be willing to acknowledge that you aren't always right and that sometimes you will make mistakes or be wrong about the information you think you received.
6. Be a lifelong learner and educate yourself on many topics.
7. Increase your vocabulary. When speaking to spirits, you're communicating in a different language and translating what you receive into your native language. The larger your vocabulary, the easier it will be to translate those messages accurately and with the proper nuances so you're using the best possible words. As Samuel Clemens (Mark Twain) said, "The difference between the *almost* right word and the *right* word is really a large matter. 'Tis the difference between the lightning bug and the lightning."

A word of caution: Please don't play around with Ouija boards or seances or lighting candles and chanting. And please never make pacts with demons or demonic beings. Demonic beings want to destroy everything they touch. They'll lie and promise you anything to get you under their control. I talk more about demons in chapter 7.

Don't offer to make sacrifices to any being—none of the beings I've communicated with, including many divine beings from many traditions and cultures, have ever asked for a sacrifice, nor do they want it. If a being asks you for a sacrifice, they are almost certainly impostors and not who they say they are. All these practices can be effective, but mainly effective in attracting the wrong kind of spirit.

## *Some of the dead want our help*

It's commonly believed that those who have left physical life are watching over us and are helping us from where they are.

And some of them are and do, though most of the helpful ones have only limited power and can mostly only send you messages of hope and comfort, or pray on your behalf from where they are, asking that you be protected and kept safe on earth.

But many of them can't or don't want to help. Instead, they may need our help, even if they don't know it.

Imagine you had a crotchety great uncle who was verbally abusive and drove everyone away with his attitude. Suppose further that while he lived in physical reality, anyone who asked him for help was refused, perhaps self-righteously, with an attendant lecture on pulling yourself up by your bootstraps or how he made his own way and expects everyone else to do the same.

Maybe he was that way because of his own unrecognized and therefore unresolved family trauma. Or maybe he was just naturally like that.

When that uncle left this earth, he didn't suddenly become a gracious, generous, enlightened being. He's still the same crotchety person; he just isn't in a body anymore.

If he treated others badly enough, he's likely in the special school I've talked about.

If he's interested in becoming a better human being, he's got all the opportunities and help he needs in the afterlife. But until he learns to be a better being, he remains focused on his own needs and he doesn't have any power to help anyone on earth. He doesn't have the bandwidth to focus on anyone else, nor does he want to. With enough gentle education in the special school, he may choose to become a better soul and may start to care about others, but for now, he's still a curmudgeon and has no desire, nor any ability, to help anyone still living in physical reality.

However, although he has no power to help you, you have the power to help him. You can pray for him—though not in a "make this terrible uncle a better person" way—I don't agree with that coercive approach to prayer.

Instead, you can pray for him to receive the appropriate help, the type of help that he can recognize and accept. He's got that help anyway—he's surrounded with it—but your prayers will help those around him help him see it more clearly.

One final note: Whenever you talk about anyone or anything, you are invoking that person or being's presence. They know you're talking about them. They might not consciously know, yet they know on a more important, deeper, energetic level. With some beings, however, they know consciously, and they will come. I'll repeat that: They will come. This is why I won't say certain names—I don't want to invoke them into my presence. For that reason, I caution you to be careful who and what you invoke.

This means that if you speak of anyone, including the dearly departed, they will know and your words will affect them for good or ill. Perhaps this is why we have the saying about only speaking good of the dead. Let's say a public figure, a living person, is endlessly invoked by name with ill or good wishes. That onslaught of energy affects them. The same applies to the dearly departed—everything you think and say about them is sent to them energetically. It's unfair to them. I recommend that if you are feeling ill wishes toward someone, that you do your best to summon compassion and understanding for them and not send them any more bad energy than they're already receiving. Remember that everyone goes to heaven, no exceptions, and everyone is met with infinite mercy and justice when they get there. Even if they are a horrible human being while in a physical body, they will face the music once they die, though in a gentle, compassionate, and understanding way, and they may eventually learn to be a better human being.

And doesn't it feel better in your heart to release, however you can, the anger and hatred you feel toward someone? If they're dead, they know they did wrong. If they're alive, they know it now or they will figure it out once they get to the afterlife. Meanwhile, you can unburden your heart by letting go of energetically attacking people you don't like. I'm not saying you must approve of them or like them. As I said earlier, and as I discuss in chapter 6, you can't force yourself to feel emotions, nor should you try. Just let go of attacking others. Defending yourself is a basic human right, and if you need to defend yourself, that's another matter. But you can defend yourself without attack, and that's what I advocate.

# Chapter 6
# Emotions in heaven and on earth

If you're under the misapprehension, as I once was, that there are no emotions in heaven, consider this: love is an emotion. The Divine loves us. Why would the Divine take away our ability to love after we leave our physical bodies? How loving would that be? How could we possibly advance as spiritual beings without love?

I learned the importance of emotions in my early years of listening to and talking with my guides and other beings, including people who have left their physical bodies.

On October 30, 1991 (coincidentally, exactly thirty-two years ago as I write this chapter), an author who had died a few years before came to me and asked me to pass a message on to his wife. He said he was in a kind of school that he called urunu. At the time, I had never heard of the school he spoke of, and I don't know even today whether the school he was talking about was the same as the special school I see others in. It didn't seem it was; it seemed more like an exciting place where he was learning new skills. But I was so new to communicating with discarnate beings then, and had so much to learn, that I didn't know the right questions to ask.

I never passed the message along to his wife. I didn't know her, though she lived in a nearby city. I just couldn't see myself, a stranger, approaching her and saying, "Your husband sent a message to you through me." Yeah, that would go over so well. I wasn't courageous enough to try, though I always wondered whether something good might have arisen out of trying to get the message to her. She died in 2003 and I am sure she got the message directly from him after she died. But still.

When speaking with the author, I felt a huge sense of sorrow and regret coming from him. I told him that I felt like crying. The author apologized and said, "It is me—a reaction to my emotions. I am sorry for letting them through like that. I miss her." (As a side note, notice how he instantly takes responsibility. Responsibility is integral to the afterlife, and that's why I discuss it throughout this book.)

Surprised, I said, "I thought there weren't supposed to be emotions there." Because I, like many other people, had the misunderstanding that our emotions are all bad, or that they are an earthly, physical-body type of experience that has nothing to do with the spiritual. In that way of thinking, once we get to the afterlife, all emotions go away. This belief is a secret relief to many people. The thinking goes something like this: If all emotions go away in the afterlife, you don't have to do the hard, messy, and sometimes complicated work of learning to work with them.

When I said to the author that I didn't think there were emotions in the afterlife, Seth, a non-physical spirit who had contacted me early on and had been coaching me in how to communicate with spirit beings, answered in a booming voice, "A misunderstanding indeed!"

And that's when I started to learn the importance of emotions. Since then, I've learned a lot about emotions. Once I dropped the belief that there are no emotions in the afterlife, I instantly saw the illogic of that belief, an illogic I stated at the start of this chapter and in chapter 3. It bears repeating: How can we believe in love, which is an emotion, and think that the Divine loves us, if we think that emotions aren't a part of our existence as souls, and aren't a part of the existence of other spiritual beings? Let's look at this more closely.

## *What's important about emotions?*

When you think about it, love, one of the most important things in our entire multidimensional existence, is an emotion. So how can we say emotions are bad? You might respond that some emotions are bad and some are good, but I contend that all emotions are needed and therefore good. I don't understand emotions well, but I know they are enormously important and are an essential part of our being, not just while we're in our bodies, but before and after too. We need emotions for our spiritual growth and advancement. Our emotions aren't bad, but we can sometimes do bad things because we aren't handling our emotions properly and responsibly. When you first experience what a clean anger feels like, you suddenly understand the difference.

What do I mean by clean anger? Or clean emotions in general? I mean emotions that aren't overladen with the desire to harm or manipulate others, and that aren't overladen with subtext and unconscious thoughts. A clean anger is an appropriate response to something, either something being done to yourself or something being done to someone you care about. When experiencing a clean anger, you might shout, but you don't lash out; you behave responsibly and accept responsibility for your actions.

One story from the Christian Bible relates that Jesus, being hungry, seeks fruit from a fig tree. The tree he tries has only leaves, so he gets angry at a fig tree for not bearing fruit, and subsequently curses it. That story puzzled me for a long time—what did the tree do (or not do) to deserve being cursed? When I asked the Divine for an explanation, the answer was instant. As with most stories about Jesus, it's an analogy. The fig tree's purpose is to bear figs, yet the tree wasn't fulfilling its purpose. Just so, we humans have our purposes. Some purposes are simply to exist and, by existing and being the best person we know how to be, contribute to the welfare and happiness of those we encounter; other purposes require work from us. Aside from simply existing, if we don't do our work and therefore don't fulfill our purpose, we are failing those who rely on us. (There are more meanings to the story of the fig tree, but I've never seen this aspect mentioned.)

In contrast to clean anger, the other kind of anger (and other emotions) could be called dirty anger or dirty emotions. People experiencing dirty anger lash out at others; attack people verbally or physically; don't think about what their responsibilities are and therefore don't act responsibly. Such people often use their anger as an excuse for whatever harm they did. "I'm sorry I called you names, but I didn't mean it; I was angry." No, they did mean it, and they used their anger to lash out at you in the same way people use their drunkenness as an excuse for their poor behavior. There's a reason the ancient Latin phrase, *in vino, veritas,* is still popular. It translates as "in wine, there is truth," and means that what people say when drunk is what they truly are thinking, thoughts they hide when sober. Likewise, people who are drunk on their anger use it as an excuse to lash out, claiming afterwards that their anger made them do it. That's dirty anger.

## *Handling emotions appropriately*

The key to emotions is to not let them overwhelm you and to not think you are your emotions. You *experience* emotions, you aren't your emotions. You experience fear or hate or love or worry or warmth or compassion or any number of other emotions; you aren't those things.

It's usually easy to experience the "good" emotions such as compassion or love; it's harder to experience grief, fear, or anger.

Emotions are supposed to move, like water. If you try to stifle the more difficult emotions, they harden, like ice, and stick around. Emotions aren't supposed to stick around. When they harden and thicken and become immobile, they harm you, and you may choose to harm others because you're not correctly handling your emotions.

*Figure 16. Handling your emotions takes skill. To keep from being overwhelmed, don't let yourself drown in them but instead stay on top of them, like a boat on water.*

The next time you experience an emotion, whether comfortable or uncomfortable, rather than letting yourself drown in it, try surfing it, like you're surfing a wave, or try riding on top of it, like you're rafting a river. Observe the emotion and what it brings to you, and what it brings you to. You are experiencing that emotion; you are not that emotion. For example, you are *experiencing* fear; you are *not* fear. It could help to focus on your breathing as you do so.

To be more aware of our emotions, and more in control of how we handle them, cognitive science research advises naming what you're feeling: "I am feeling fear. I am feeling despair. I am feeling sad." Our emotions are centered in the amygdala part of our brain, the emotion center where it's hard to deal rationally with emotions. Naming our emotions moves our focus to the prefrontal cortex part of our brain, where we can more rationally think about and deal with those emotions.

Eventually, as you name and ride atop your emotions, the emotion change and take you to a different place, a place where you'll receive a gift.

This process is easy to describe, but hard to learn. I assure you that, as with any skill, it gets easier with practice. If you don't get it the first time or the first few or many times you try it, keep at it. Eventually you'll find yourself handling your emotions more smoothly.

I'm not advocating denying your emotions, or shoving them aside, and especially not acting them out on other people. Instead, I'm recommending that you accept and observe your emotions with a certain amount of detachment from them. If your emotions overwhelm you, consult with a counselor or faith leader.

### *Handling an emotional piggybacker*

Here's a dirty little secret many people have. Many people aren't willing to be responsible and do their inner work of handling their own emotions, so they find the closest unshielded, sensitive, empathic person and shove their emotions over to that person. Most aren't consciously aware they're doing this, but they do it nonetheless. It's a form of emotional abuse, and as a psychic, I've seen it often. This practice has two primary problems:

1. When someone does this, they force their emotions onto someone else, making that other person handle those emotions and do false inner work, inner work that's not their own to do, making that other person's burden heavier, and
2. It prevents the person who is shirking their responsibility from making any spiritual progress. If they don't accept responsibility for their emotions, they can't do any kind of inner work or make themselves any better than they are.

I learned about this nasty practice in my early years as a practicing psychic. At the time I had a psychic acquaintance who taught me some useful information and skills. This fact about people using others to handle their emotions was one of them. She pointed out that one sign you are taking on another's emotions is that the emotions don't feel right. I compare it with ill-fitting clothing someone snuck into your wardrobe—it seems like it's yours, but it's uncomfortable and doesn't fit you. I call this emotional piggybacking.

Another sign someone is doing this to you is if the emotions came out of the blue—one moment you are fine or relaxed or happy, and the next you're suddenly tense or grumpy or feeling some other emotion that doesn't fit the situation you're in.

My acquaintance recommended some steps to take when this happens.

First, ask yourself if those are your emotions. If the answer is "no," ask yourself whose emotions they are—who do the emotions feel like?

Most of the time, as soon as you identify the perp, they stop sending their emotions to you. It isn't that they are consciously doing this to you, but subconsciously they know they've been caught and no longer have your permission to use you, at least in that moment, so they flee.

The second thing to do when someone is trying to use you to process their emotions is to firmly and permanently withdraw permission for them to do so. They had previously gotten your permission on some level. Withdrawing your permission means they can no longer do it. What do I mean by saying they got your permission?

Because of free will, nothing can be done to us without our permission. That doesn't mean we consciously say to someone, "Oh, yeah, sure, you can use me as your emotional punching bag!" But we can be persuaded in all manner of devious ways to give our permission on the soul level. For example, you might have felt compassion for that person, and you might have believed that it was your responsibility to help them; that you could somehow help them do their inner work; that if you only love them enough and sacrifice yourself enough, you could somehow "fix" them or save them or heal them. That belief was the permission they needed to take advantage of you. This is often the mechanism of unconscious permission; when someone comes along and energetically knocks on our door, offering their uncomfortable emotions for us to handle, we say "Sure, hand it over!"

Another way we give permission is believing we don't deserve any better, so when someone wants to abuse us, we let them.

Again, none of this is on the conscious level, though as we continue our inner work, we grow more conscious of these mechanisms. This growth is yet another reason to commit to doing our inner work and, if we repeatedly find ourselves in situations where someone is using and abusing us, to seek help from a faith leader or counselor.

## *How emotional piggybacking works*

It might not seem obvious at first, but this practice of using others to take on our emotions is related to the afterlife, so bear with me while I explain the mechanism.

Let's say that Uncle Bob isn't comfortable with certain emotions because he associates those emotions with being weak or helpless. Maybe Bob doesn't like feeling helpless or uncertain, or doesn't like feeling irritated, or Bob has a problem with rage.

Rather than sit with those emotions and flow with them to see where they take him on a journey of self-discovery, Bob repudiates those emotions. He chooses to push them onto and into the nearest empathetic person for them to handle.

How does that look? Let's say you're Uncle Bob's niece (or some other relative or a friend or acquaintance), and you're an empathetic person. You notice what people are going through and you care for them, and you wish you could help them. You might even go a step further and feel obligated to help everyone. (In case you don't yet know this, you're not. As the saying goes, don't set yourself on fire to keep others warm.)

On a level of awareness below the conscious level, Uncle Bob feels irritated at something, but he doesn't want to feel that irritation. He notices, again not on the conscious level, that you, his niece, are open energetically because of your love of and sympathy for him and your desire to help. He takes advantage of you by sending his irritation to you. Uncle Bob doesn't need to be physically close to you to take advantage of you this way, and in fact it's better from his point of view if he isn't, because people who don't know about this kind of psychic invasion are unlikely to put two and two together and come up with the answer "Bob." That is, if Bob were in your presence and you noticed he was getting irritated, then suddenly he stopped being irritated and you started being irritated, you might connect the two and realize you were feeling Bob's irritation. But if Bob isn't present, you won't know Bob's state and you won't realize there's a connection.

As soon as Uncle Bob pushes his irritation (or other emotions) away from himself and sends them to you, suddenly you feel irritated and you don't know why. But because you are feeling irritated in your mind and body, you think it's *your* irritation. If it were genuinely your irritation, and if you're a responsible person, you would deal with that irritation without sending it on to someone else and without taking it out on those around you. You may say to others, "I'm feeling a bit cranky, so I'm going to take a break," or some similar statement letting those around you know your mood. And then you take care of the irritation in whatever way you do. The same goes for dealing with an emotional piggy backer—you deal with the false emotions thinking they are yours.

*Figure 17. Uncle Bob, unwilling to handle his own emotions, shoves them onto the nearest empathetic person.*

But Uncle Bob pushing his emotions onto you puts an unwarranted burden on you, and Uncle Bob gets off scot free.

Or does he?

Let's ignore the physical ailments that can arise from undealt-with emotions—I'm not qualified to write that book, and many others are and have: for one example, see Bessel van der Kolk's *The Body Keeps the Score: Brain, Mind, and Body in the Healing of Trauma* (Penguin Books, 2014). The consequence of ignoring our emotions and not working on ourselves is not just that we don't advance spiritually, in just the same way as possession stops your spiritual growth and that of the possessor, but also that we can suffer physical ailments. (I talk about possession in chapter 13.)

If Uncle Bob continues this kind of irresponsibility, you can be sure he's going to end up in the special school after his body dies. Of course, he can continue to stagnate in the special afterlife school and not work on himself, but why would anyone not want to move on, especially when surrounded by the absolute assurance of infinite justice, love, and mercy? (I ask that, but indeed some people make exactly that choice. Why? Because they're afraid of facing themselves.)

## *Stopping emotional piggybackers*

You may be wondering, how do you stop Uncle Bob's invasiveness in the here and now?

The first thing to do is be as knowledgeable about yourself and as self-aware as you can. Easy to say, but unfortunately that's about one of the hardest things to do. Brain scientists say that although we are all conscious, few of us are self-aware. So how do you become self-aware? By paying attention to your thoughts and actions, and thinking about what they tell you about yourself. Also read about boundaries, and learn what is and isn't your responsibility. That ongoing practice will last your entire life. As you work at it, at a certain point you feel yourself becoming more aware.

To stop emotional piggybackers: Let's say you know yourself well enough to know that being irritated at nothing isn't common for you. You then ask yourself, "Whose irritation does this feel like?" You'll normally get an instant answer: "Uncle Bob. This feels like Uncle Bob."

Often, the recognition is enough. Uncle Bob knows on some level that the jig is up and he withdraws his emotions from you (then sends them to someone less aware). But what if the recognition doesn't work, and Bob keeps sending his emotions to you? Then you escalate. You mentally thank Uncle Bob for trusting you enough to share his emotions with you, adding, "But no thank you. I don't want these emotions. These are yours. I return them to you to take care of." Do this as neutrally as you can; it doesn't help anyone to send your anger to Bob for his lack of responsibility and self-control.

What if you don't recognize who it is? That's trickier. You could be being used by someone you don't know; say, if you're at a gathering with strangers present. Or it could be someone who you only know slightly, so you don't realize who it is. In those cases, do the escalation anyway: Thank whomever it is for trusting you enough to share their emotions, then tell them "No thanks."

Sometimes you might be picking up someone's emotions intuitively. That's not the same as someone using you to process their emotions. Instead, you're reading the room. You're sensitive enough to know that Uncle Bob is distressed about something, even if he's not saying anything. Maybe people are afraid of Uncle Bob's temper, so they walk on eggshells around him. If your relationship with Uncle Bob is good, you can gently ask him questions to see if he's aware of how he's feeling and how he's affecting those around him. Many people don't want to control others through fear and don't want people walking on eggshells around them; your questions might be their first step in becoming more self-aware.

But be careful doing this. If Uncle Bob is habitually angry and lashes out, and doesn't accept responsibility for himself or enjoys playing the victim, you may want to consult with a counselor or faith leader to see whether you should say anything to Uncle Bob, and if so, how to approach him. "Fixing" Uncle Bob is nobody's responsibility but his. If you want to try to help, be sure you are coming from a neutral place with no expectation of change. If you don't get far with him, let it drop and let him be who he wants to be. If he's harming you and is unwilling to acknowledge that, distance yourself.

The more you practice recognizing other people's emotions and sending them back to their source, the easier it gets to see and handle it.

## *Emotional assault*

A corollary of this type of emotional advantage-taking is when someone energetically pushes their emotions onto someone else. I don't mean in the way I just described, where one person wants another person to handle their emotions. I mean a process of emotional assault.

Because many of us haven't been taught that our emotions are okay, we don't learn how to handle our emotions. Feeling some emotions (sometimes feeling any emotions) can feel like riding a wild mustang. We think we have no control, and that all we can do is hang on for dear life. Because we aren't properly taught about emotions, if we are irresponsible, we lash out at others in a variety of ways, one of those ways being sending our emotions—anger, grief, confusion, and so on—to others to handle in the way I just described as emotional piggybacking.

But there's another way people misuse their emotions. Instead of emotional piggybacking, such people energetically attack others with their emotions. We don't do either of these things consciously; most people are unconscious of their decision to send their emotions to others (emotional piggybacking) or to attack people with their emotions.

Have you ever been around someone who was angry, who never touched you physically, but around whom you felt physically ill, like you were punched in the gut? That was them not being responsible for their emotions and using those emotions to attack you. This happens most often when someone is angry at someone else. The angry person might express their anger verbally or they might not, but they energetically push their anger onto the person they're angry at. It's like punching that other person in the stomach. Just as we can be attacked verbally, we can be attacked energetically.

As I explained earlier, anger can be clean and an appropriate response to a situation. But let's say you're angry at someone because you couldn't control that person. And let's say that, rather than acknowledge your own desire to control, and rather than acknowledge that your anger is arising out of the underlying fear you feel when you can't control those around you, you instead lash out at the other person to make them toe the line.

But you don't just lash out at them verbally; you also blast them energetically with your anger. (I'm not going to talk about physically lashing out; everyone knows that's wrong.) Blasting people with your energy isn't responsible. It's not a clean way to handle your emotions. You are harming them just as much as if you had hit them physically. The difference is that when you express your anger responsibly and keep your emotions clean, the person you express yourself to knows you're angry, but isn't hit by your energies. When you're not responsible, those you are attacking both know you're angry and are hit by your energies.

The person receiving that attack of anger might feel like they're being hit in their solar plexus, or they may feel uncomfortable all over under their skin, or they may feel like they've been hit in some other way. They feel like they've been attacked because they have been. And it isn't just anger that people attack with; it can be other emotions as well, such as grief or despair or other things with darker intentions. Though it's usually anger with an underlying foundation of fear.

Many people are perfectly capable of being angry and not shoving their anger at others in an attack, and of not using others to process their emotions. I refer to those people as having clean energy, which I discussed earlier. People with clean energy are more common than you might think. It just takes a minimum level of self-responsibility, and it doesn't require conscious thought; just the intention to be responsible for ourselves and to not attack others.

When I talk about someone having "clean" energies, I don't mean people who are in some impossible, never-angry state (which usually means denying a large part of themselves), but someone who freely allows themselves to feel all their emotions, takes responsibility for those emotions, and doesn't force them onto others.

The person pushing their emotions at another is not accepting responsibility for themselves or their emotions, and they are attacking others with their emotional energy.

## *Why are emotions important in the afterlife?*

Why is the use and misuse of emotions relevant to the topic of what comes after bodily death? Because, as I said in an earlier chapter, the training wheels come off when we die. We are no longer semi-protected by the slowness of energetic responses in the physical realm. Instead, in the afterlife, we are subject to instant responses to our impulses. In the afterlife, if we were to be irresponsible and feel anger toward someone, and as a result have a destructive impulse to lash out at someone, that someone would instantly feel the effects. But that sort of thing isn't allowed in the afterlife. Therefore, people who don't handle their emotions responsibly in physical life can and must be kept separate in the afterlife until they learn to be responsible.

The good news is that we can all start learning to be more responsible now, while still on earth living in physical reality, both in terms of not attacking others and in terms of recognizing when we're being attacked and not accepting the attack.

If you want to learn how to recognize verbal attacks (and many such attacks are quite subtle), read Suzette Haden Elgin's excellent book, *The Gentle Art of Verbal Self-Defense* (Barnes & Noble Books, 1993). She teaches how to recognize a verbal attack (for example, it's an attack if someone says to you, "If you *really* loved me, you would do X"; the attack is that they are saying you don't really love them), and how to respond appropriately. Ms. Elgin based her book on Virginia Satir's five communication modes, which I also recommend looking into.

Another good book is Eric Berne's *Games People Play: The Psychology of Human Relationships* (Grove Press, 1964). The book describes the kinds of manipulative mind games people play with each other. One simple example: Person A complains about a problem they have. Person B offers a solution. Person A responds with, "Yes, but..." and gives reasons why that solution won't work. Person B proposes another solution, which Person A says "Yes, but..." to. Person A can carry this on endlessly; they aren't interested in a solution, they're interested in seeing how long they can control Person B.

### *Becoming a better human being means accepting responsibility for ourselves*

On earth, a big part of becoming a better human being is learning to accept responsibility for ourselves and our choices, and deciding to make better choices. It's hard work and often means facing truths we'd rather not face—truths about ourself and others. Yet the work is deeply rewarding. The further down that path we go, the better this life becomes, and the better the afterlife will be.

Deciding to make better choices is key, and involves understanding and accepting that we have free will, as I described in chapter 4.

# Chapter 7
# Hell and demons

In my decades of psychic experiences and talking with those who have moved on from physical reality, I've never seen hell. I've never caught a glimpse or hint or whiff of hellfire and brimstone. I've never seen a lake of everlasting fire that people are thrown into for even one minute, let alone for eternity.

If you think about it, such a place and such a punitive attitude doesn't jibe with the concept of a Divine being who loved the idea of us so much they created us in their image. Though I understand the human desire, arising out of fear, rage, and a desire for vengeance, to imagine such a place exists—for other people, of course, and never for oneself.

The idea of eternal punishment also doesn't jibe with the idea of free will. From the Divine point of view, it wouldn't make sense to give people the freedom to choose, then punish us for our choices. That's a horrible catch-22 trap, and the Divine isn't anything close to being that way. (The term catch-22 refers to an impossible situation where rules contradict each other and therefore cannot be followed. Joseph Heller invented the term for his novel, *Catch-22*, first published by Simon & Schuster in 1961. The cynically grim novel accurately reflects some aspects of human existence. The late Sir Terry Pratchett personified this same idea in his excellent Discworld books with his invention of a group of beings he called the Auditors, who valued rules so highly that they were antithetical to life and could be defeated by nonsensical things, such as a sign that says "Go right" but points to the left. Pratchett first mentions the Auditors in *Reaper Man*, NAL, 1991.)

## *Fear, hell, and the Divine*

The Divine hasn't set us up. Wherever I look on many planes of existence, all I see is infinite justice, infinite love, and infinite mercy. Before we sang the physical universe into existence, when we were created, we were all given free will so we could enjoy our existence. With free will, we can choose our own adventure; we can choose who we want to be and who we want to hang out with. If that means, as Jesus once said to me, hanging out with the riffraff in the pool hall of the souls, so be it. (Although he didn't recommend that for me, he held no judgment for anyone making that choice.)

More likely, some person or persons invented the idea of hell to justify their bad behavior toward others and to control others through fear. If you can convince people that everything that's most natural and good about life is sinful, and, if indulged in, condemns you to everlasting fire, you put them into a catch-22. They can't prevent themselves from being human and doing human things, but **they are in a torment of fear for being human.** This raises misplaced anger in their hearts against the Divine for asking the impossible of them. This anger disconnects them from the Divine, which is certainly one reason some people try to convince others that their natural human state is a sin. Disconnect people from having a direct relationship with the Divine, and you disconnect them from a wellspring of comfort and advice and guidance on what the real right thing to do is.

Here's an example of how fearful of the Divine people can become. An acquaintance once invited me to attend a hand bell-ringing ceremony at a Christian church in Santa Rosa, California.

The ceremony was lovely and profoundly moving. While enjoying the ceremony, I reached out to Jesus and asked him if he was also enjoying it. I had to reach quite far to find him.

"Why are you so far away?" I asked him. (I asked psychically, of course! Not aloud.)

His answer surprised me.

"Because the people in this church are terrified of me. If I come any closer, they'll sense my presence and will go further into fear, and I don't want my presence to terrify them even more. Giving people cause to be more fearful isn't a loving act."

He also explained that not only were all those people terrified of him, they were also hugely, deeply resentful toward God, and many were angry, some to the point of rage, at God.

For all the lip service given to Jesus being a loving being, the people in that church were secretly terrified that Jesus was some vengeful, perfect being who would punish and blast them for being imperfect, horrible people. Being human, with human desires and flaws, equated to being horrible humans in their minds.

Given how people are taught by other human beings, it makes sense that many Christians secretly fear Jesus and many people, despite their religion, secretly fear their Divine beings, whomever they worship. (Though in my experience, pagans tend to have more relaxed and respectful relationships with their divine beings.)

This fear of Divine beings isn't just in the Christian religion; it's also in many other religions. There's often a big difference between what a religion officially believes and what its followers believe it is about. Although the core teaching of many religions is to treat each other with loving kindness (with many variations on the theme of "do unto others as you would have them do unto you"), the most common teachings, the teachings people tell each other about their religions, are that "we must all be perfect or else." The injunction is usually accompanied by a hugely long list of "thou shalt nots," often catch-22 types of injunctions,that we must obey to be acceptable to the Divine.

One common example of such a catch-22 injunction goes something like this: "Thou shalt abhor and abjure sex, but once you are married, sex is sacred and holy." How is someone supposed to make the shift from feeling guilty for their natural and normal sexual desires *before* marriage to feeling okay about those desires *after* marriage, especially when we've been indoctrinated since infancy into feeling guilty about our natural human desires? We can't, not without lots of outside help and counseling, which most people don't even realize they need, let alone get.

What those teachings really mean is we must not be human for us to be acceptable to (and controllable by) the human beings teaching us to fear the Divine.

Many religious folks teach us that we must be perfect or the Divine won't love us, while at the same time saying that if we bend our necks to our faith leaders and to what those leaders teach, we have a chance of escaping Divine punishment.

Because people know in their hearts they aren't perfect, they aren't saints, and sometimes they fail at being reasonably good human beings, they live in a ferment of fear and self-loathing and anger at themselves and at a Divine being who has given them an impossible task.

But they're focusing on the wrong target. In religious texts from any religion that I've studied, none of the various gods and goddesses have ever asked anyone to be perfect as we humans define it. Nor have any of the gods and goddesses I've spoken with ever asked for sacrifices or worship. Instead, they have all asked for clear, honest communication, and have expressed a desire to develop a closer relationship with us human beings. And those deities sure aren't judging any of us or punishing any of us or sending us into a torment of eternal damnation.

The only judgment is coming from our fellow human beings. The teachings that tell us we are all going to hell and that none of us can ever be good enough for a supreme being come from our fellow human beings. The idea that a supreme being forces us to do bad things comes from human beings. The idea that a supreme being causes bad things to happen comes from human beings.

## *What about people you think deserve hell?*

Let's address the elephant in the room. How did you feel when I said everyone goes to heaven, regardless of what they've done, and that no one goes to hell? Did you feel relieved? Or are you angry because you think somebody you know deserves eternal punishment? Do you desire vengeance? I can't speak for you, though I know how it feels to hate someone so deeply that you wish them ill. Revenge stories (most of them made up) are hugely popular on the internet for a reason.

But I will ask that you sit with those feelings and see where they take you. (As I advised in chapter 6 when I spoke of handling your emotions.) If you feel that some people deserve hell because they behaved badly, where does that stop? At what level of bad behavior does someone stop deserving Divine redemption and forgiveness and start becoming completely irredeemable? I'm not saying *you* must forgive them. I am saying that everyone is Divinely forgiven and forgivable, no matter how horribly they behave or how many people they harm. As I describe in this chapter, we are all forgivable and redeemable, even demons.

## *Which version of the Bible?*

I'll address an objection I've encountered: The objection is that the Bible (both the Hebrew Bible or, as Christians call it, the Old Testament, and the Christian Bible, which Christians call the New Testament) is God's inerrant word and is to be taken literally, and that the Bible is filled with references to hell. This claim is arguable and exaggerated; the few references to hell have been challenged by thoughtful and educated scholars as not being about a spiritual place of punishment, or at least not being a place of punishment for humans, but instead is only for a specific demon.

This belief in hell is usually accompanied by the belief that God has somehow lost the ability to speak to modern people, and so therefore, anyone claiming to be talking to God today is lying and probably Satan's pawn. If you're a Christian and your faith leaders have taught you this, be aware that Christians do not universally hold either of these beliefs. Catholics believe that hell exists but is a choice and a state of being; it's *self-exclusion* from communion with God. And many Catholics believe that no one is in hell. Pope Francis said, speaking as a human being and not as the pope, that he liked to think hell is empty.

And many people, Christian and other, quietly believe that they hold conversations with God and there's nothing demonic about it, For that matter, prayer is a conversation with God, so it's a contradiction to believe that nobody can talk with God and God doesn't listen to or talk with us.

Furthermore, the message we are often told is that we all need to listen to the various fallible religious leaders who tell us what *they* think the Bible says and what it means; we aren't to think for ourselves what the Bible means.

The same is true for the belief that the Bible is the inerrant word of god and is to be taken literally: Faith leaders who are more interested in controlling us than in leading us teach this. (Because even though Jesus spoke in analogy and parables, God never speaks allegorically?) Not all Christians hold this belief, either.

But even if you accept the literalness and inerrancy of the Bible as your truth, which version of the Bible does this apply to? Which version is the inerrant word of God? For some people, it's new information to find that there is more than one version of the Bible. For example, I met a Christian who had never heard of any other version than the King James version, and when I told her it was just one translation among many, she was offended and horrified. It can come as a surprise to find that things you were told are in the Bible aren't, in fact, there, or were added later (such as to the King James version).

*Figure 18. We have many versions of the Hebrew and Christian Bibles, not just one. And that's not even touching on other holy books from other religions.*

And which texts do you trust? Older or later versions? Versions that were extent shortly after Jesus's time, but declared hundreds of years later as not cannon, apocryphal, or even heretical? (For a peek into how modern Christianity was shaped by politics early on, look up the Council of Nicea.)

If you want to learn more about what scholars now know about the various versions of the Bible and whether you can trust those versions as being unadulterated by later writers, read any of Bart D. Ehrman's books; for example, *Forged: Writing in the Name of God—Why the Bible's Authors Are Not Who We Think They Are* (HarperOne, 2011). Just keep in mind that archaeologists continue to discover new texts and scholars continue to figure out more about ancient languages.

If you'd like to read translations of ancient myths from which much of the Hebrew Bible was constructed, I recommend *Hebrew Myths*, by Robert Graves and Raphael Patai, who are respectively a Protestant and a Jew (Doubleday, 1963).

For a more accurate Bible translation than the King James version, I highly recommend Ferrar Fenton's *The Holy Bible in Modern English* (Destiny Publishers, 1966). For your amusement and edification, I recommend looking up the confrontation between Moses and the Pharaoh in Fenton's translation.

## *My visit to the outer darkness*

Having said I've never seen anything resembling hell, nonetheless I've seen and experienced a place I call the outer darkness. Some might call it hell, but it isn't a place the Divine throws us into as a punishment, nor is it a lake of fire. Instead, the outer darkness is a dark, featureless, nonphysical place on the edges of our greater reality where souls go who have walked far down a dark path, and where souls are sometimes thrust by others.

I once found myself in the outer darkness—not in my physical body, but as my soul self. I didn't know why I was there, though many years later, I realized I was pushed there by someone who wished me ill. (I think I know who, but there's no reason to name names.)

In this place, I was lying on my back in a puddle of dim light surrounded by a textured darkness. Far behind me was a boundary between the place of light and life and the darkness I was within. I sensed malevolent beings moving in the darkness on the edges of my puddle of light.

I couldn't easily move on my own volition. Instead, I was moved around by unseen energies, and it felt like I was being dragged by some impersonal force. Any movement I tried pushed me further away from the light and deeper and downward into the darkness.

It was frightening. I felt terrified, bereft, and abandoned, as I had felt throughout my entire childhood. As I slid further into the darkness, and as the malevolencies in the darkness surrounding me moved closer, I silently cried out for help from my heart.

**I didn't know it then, but all we ever need to do is ask for help, and it is given**. Such requests for help are a form of prayer. Prayers don't need to be by the book; they can be and often are formed in the heart. We must ask for help, though; it can't come unbidden to us. That's because help given without a request, and therefore without consent, would override someone's free will. If you've received help and don't feel you asked for it, you either asked for it in a way you don't remember, or someone asked for help on your behalf and you unconsciously agreed with that request.

And if you're wondering how someone could override my free will enough to push me into this place, they didn't. Overriding someone's free will is impossible. However, you can get around someone's conscious desires by appealing to their subconscious beliefs about themselves. If you try to harm someone and on some level that person believes they deserve harm, they'll let you harm them. If you're wondering how someone else had the power to send me there, it's because at the time, because of my childhood, I believed I didn't deserve to live.

As soon as I cried for help, I was lifted out and away from that sere, sterile darkness and was returned to life.

I don't think that place, the outer darkness, is hell. I think it's a place where many souls go when they choose to separate themselves from all that is holy and good. No soul is sent there by the Divine as punishment, though sometimes souls can be sent there by other beings, as was my case.

Dante says in the *Inferno* section of his *Divine Comedy* that the only beings in hell are there by choice; that they can leave hell as soon as they repent of their bad acts. As surprised as I was to read that, I think he knew a truth. The outer darkness is a desolate, barren place devoid of light, movement, love, and sound, filled with grim sensations and beings of malevolent intent preying on each other. Yet no being is there by compulsion or as punishment; they are there because the choices they've made led them naturally and inevitably to such a place, and they can leave by making different choices.

This makes it sound like the outer darkness is, after all, some kind of punishment, but it isn't. It's a place beings find when they follow a certain path and make certain choices that, one after another, lead them to the next choice, and the next, until they find themselves deep in dark territory. (Or they're there because someone pushed them there, but that's rare.) Think of it as a location beings gravitate to rather than a place where they are confined.

## *We walk our paths one choice at a time*

As I said in chapter 4, we all have free will. We all have agency. None of us are victims. All of us can make choices either for good or ill. Those choices lead us down certain paths, and none of the paths, no matter how far we take them, are irrevocable.

I'll illustrate what I mean by using the analogy of walking through a forest. Let's further postulate that you have several places to enter the forest, places that are the trail heads for paths leading more deeply into the woods. Each trail head is a specific path that leads to specific places. Each has signposts and maybe a bulletin board declaring where the path leads and what you can expect on that path. (Though in real life we seldom have all the information we need.)

*Figure 19. Each path we take comprises a series of choices. Each choice leads us further down the path or takes us onto a new path, one we didn't see before.*

According to your nature, you carefully consider your choices, or maybe you rush hastily toward a random choice. Saint Augustine said we participate in the eternal law of reason and will; that is, that we have and make choices. Like Socrates before him, Augustine said we can discern what is good and what is evil; Socrates said no one needs to teach us those things. So as we consider our paths, we are also weighing the good versus the bad. Now, our perceptions might be distorted, so we can't see the good or bad clearly, but deep inside, we know what's right and what's wrong. We may choose a bad path because we selfishly see it benefits us, even if it doesn't benefit anyone else, and even if it actively harms others. We know when we make that choice that it's a poor choice, but we make it anyway. In the long run, we can learn from our choices and, if we grow as human beings, we can learn to make better choices.

In this analogy of walking through a forest, once you've committed to a path, you follow it as it rises and falls, twists and turns. As you walk, you enjoy the scenery and make further choices when the path divides. The further you go down your chosen path, the further away you are from your starting point. It could be your starting point was good and now the path is getting even better; or the opposite could be true—the starting point was bad and each choice is taking you down a worsening path.

As you climb hills on your path or dip into valleys, you see new sights and make new choices. When you start walking, you might think the path is leading you to one place, but as you travel, you see something further down the path you didn't expect. Maybe you change your plans and head in that new direction. Maybe you feel guilty for leaving the initial path, thinking you should have stayed on that path no matter what, but you would never have seen the new path unless you'd traveled far enough down the original path.

Now let's say you reach a point where you're tired of the path and you want to go back. Maybe you see the destructiveness inherent in your path, or see that it's not fulfilling you. You might be tempted to think, "Well, I've invested so much into walking this path that I should keep going." But that's illogical; it's called the sunk cost fallacy. The sunk cost fallacy is when, even when it's clear that it would be better to abandon your path, you don't want to because you've invested so much in it. So even though you are continuing to do the equivalent of throwing good money after bad, you continue to pursue a course of action because you don't want to lose what you've already invested. But because you'll lose everything you invest, not just the amount you've invested so far, it's illogical to continue investing in a bad course of action.

Let's say you see the illogic of continuing to pursue a path. Or maybe it's become so painful to you, mentally, emotionally, or spiritually, that you can no longer bear it. You can't just suddenly be back at your starting point. No, just as you got to this point one step at a time, you must also return one step at a time. It can be hard work, though deeply satisfying, to walk away from an unhappy path and make progress on a new, happier path, but it's worth it. If we choose to learn from every action we take, and from the consequences of those actions, we can take joy in our progress toward being better souls.

That's the case for demons. Demons are a different type of soul than human, souls who have free will just as we all do, who have chosen evil. They've gone so far down their demony path, they must travel a long way to get back out of demon land.

It's hard for anyone, including demons, to retrace their steps far enough back to start on a new path. But it's not impossible, and of the many demons I've spoken with, most are relieved to be told that it's possible to chose a better path.

## *Demons and other wildlife*

In chapter 13, I speak about human souls possessing other people. Here, I talk specifically about demons.

I used to think evil didn't exist, and I didn't believe demons existed either. In my psychic practice, I discovered to my surprise that both exist. Evil exists: There are people who choose to pursue truly evil actions. Though I will never say anyone or any being is 100 percent evil, because what I've seen is that everything has a spark of the divine. It isn't possible for anything that is purely evil to exist.

And just as evil exists, so do demons. I use the word "demon" because I don't have a better word to describe them. Other cultures and religions have different terms and names for them; for example, one term is "chaos monster." Some names for chaos monsters include Tiamat, Leviathan, and so on. Many of these beings aren't evil, but have been judged to be so by believers of other religions. You can decide what you want to call them.

Although I've communicated with and sometimes wrestled with demons, I don't know much about their origins. Some say they were angels who rebelled against the Divine and were kicked out of (or fell from) heaven. I have no opinion on whether demons are fallen angels.

I believe that the idea of fallen angels is a memory of when a large group of souls (a heavenly choir) was singing physical reality into existence. Some souls in that group disagreed with the plan. I and many others argued with the dissenters and tried to convince them to rejoin the group. The more we argued, the denser the rebels became energetically, until they fell into physical reality. If you want, you can think of it as them losing their wings and becoming subject to physical reality's rules.

The group trying to convince those who fell dived in after them, trying to "save" them. And then we all got stuck in physical reality. Those of us who tried to argue the dissenters out of their rebellion should have just let them be. None of those souls were demons; they mostly have incarnated as humans throughout time. (Meaning that aspects of the greater souls that they were while singing are incarnated. See chapter 8 for my unusual take on reincarnation.)

*Figure 20. Demons did not come from the heavenly choir.*

Falling into physical reality doesn't mean any of us were angels or that those who fell were fallen angels or became demons. Your next question might be, why do I say they aren't demons? Where do I think demons come from? The answer is that souls don't just come in one flavor, with that flavor being human. In my years as a psychic, I've seen a variety of types of souls. It isn't relevant to talk in this book about the other kinds of souls I've seen and communicated with psychically. Some of them prefer that humans don't know about them. Suffice it to say that not every soul inhabiting a human-looking body is a human soul.

That's one reason why I don't believe that those who fell from the heavenly choir into physical reality are demons. It's possible that some human souls can, by dint of persistent choices for evil, eventually become demons, but I haven't seen that. Instead, I believe that demons are a separate kind of soul, neither angelic nor human, that are nonetheless sharing the same living space as we humans. They delight in wickedness, if you will, and are convinced that they are damned forever, so they think they might as well continue to harm others. But they aren't damned, and they don't have to continue to do harm.

Demons are a part of the human ecosystem—you can find them in many places on this planet, meddling in many people's lives. They control politicians, religious leaders, and the heads of many corporations, as well as other people, such as children, spouses, siblings, and so on. We can make ourselves more or less susceptible to demonic control through our choices and actions. For example, abusing drugs and alcohol opens us up to possible possession from demons and other humans.

Our denial of the existence of demons makes it easier for demons to get away with their mischief. When something is right in front of you, but you deny that it exists, you instead see what you want to see, not what's there. One clue to a demon's presence is fear—if a politician, religious leader, or company manager tries to control you through fear, there's a good chance they're in league with evil. I'm speaking from personal experiences I've had on the psychic plane with some of the demon-controlled, but I won't name names because some of the demon-controlled people are quite powerful. And although I've successfully disentangled myself from those beings, I'd rather not reopen a can of worms.

## *What about tricksters?*

When speaking about supernatural beings, many cultures have stories about tricksters. In this context, a trickster is a being who likes to play tricks on other supernatural beings and on humans. You have almost certainly heard of Loki, the Norse god and trickster, and Coyote, a famous trickster in tribal cultures in North America.

Many people dislike tricksters and even consider them to be evil, saying nothing good comes of consorting with them.

In my experience as a psychic, I disagree. I've communicated with a number of tricksters, including Loki and Coyote, as well as some unknown tricksters who are local to specific places rather than globally. By "local," I mean beings who roam a specific physical locale. When doing readings for one client, a few times I communicated with a being who identified as a trickster (one I'd never heard of) and watched over a large valley in the Eastern United States. In all my communications with tricksters, I've only experienced from them respect and a concern for my well-being; I've never experienced anything evil or worrying.

Loki once told me that even the gods evolve and that he has a mission of helping people who've experienced childhood trauma (one reason he contacted me). He's still a trickster, but in service to the good. And Coyote contacted me in her female form to give me the idea for a story of a woman suffering from and breaking free of narcissistic abuse. I turned the story into a reasonably decent screenplay that was a quarter finalist in a major screenplay competition. Writing that screenplay helped me heal a huge fear I'd had my entire life.

Some people see our stories about tricksters as moral tales; stories we can learn from. And I agree. As Joseph Campbell taught, our myths, fairy tales, and cultural stories convey a great deal of wisdom and practical knowledge about human nature. Tricksters are here to help, and sometimes they need to trick people to get past that person's rock-like beliefs that are keeping them stuck in a specific way of being.

## *Dealing with demons*

On the other hand, unlike tricksters, demons *are* evil and harbor bad intentions toward all life. Many demons influence people to do bad things to themselves and others, and some demons have taken over (possess) a person's body, often a highly placed and influential person, and run those people to wreak havoc on a larger scale. This idea is brilliantly illustrated in the 2023 movie, *The Pope's Exorcist*, which is based on Father Gabriele Amorth's first two books, *An Exorcist Tells His Story* (Ignatius Press, 1999) and *An Exorcist: More Stories* (Ignatius Press, 2002). The books and movie are quite accurate, though I disagree with the approach taken to remove demons. The good father fiercely fought the demons he confronted, but I've found that compassion and understanding work equally well and maybe even better. (With the exception of a few stubborn, recalcitrant demons who might only be able to be moved away from tormenting someone through exorcism.)

It isn't obvious when someone is influenced by demons, and recognizing that they are is further hindered by a lack of belief in demons. If we don't believe in something, and we see the results of that something's works, we are more likely to attribute those results to something else. It's a form of denial, and when we deny something, we hide from ourselves not only the existence of that something, but also the ability to effectively deal with it. I speak more about this in a few paragraphs.

I said earlier I use the term "demon" because that's the closest word I know. It might be useful to describe what I see when I encounter demons.

Demons have no specific appearance; they come in different shapes, colors, and sizes. I've seen large ones who look typically demonic; their exterior is a blackish red. I've seen smaller demons the size of rabbits who are gray. When I was in college, I psychically saw a demon forming in my living room who looked like a typical satyr; the pupils of their eyes were rectangles, like a goat's pupils, only vertical and not horizontal, and their pupils were yellow while the rest of their eyes were black. I was terrified and years away from being able to defend myself against this kind of being; I climbed through my bedroom window and fled.

Demons are who and what they are because of a series of choices that moved them inexorably, step by step, choice by choice, further away from the divine presence. They aren't banned or banished or cast into the fires of hell; they dwell in a dark spiritual place that enfolds and surrounds them that, like in Dante's *Inferno*, is of their own choosing. They are there because they chose to be there and continue to choose to be there until they change their mind. This dwelling place is energy, not a location, which is why demons can roam physical reality and wreak havoc wherever they go.

Demons are dedicated to evil and do their best to influence people to do evil as well. One of the ways they get away with this mischief is through people's disbelief in evil and in demons specifically. As long as someone says evil doesn't exist and that demons (whatever word you want to use for them) don't exist, you won't recognize the source of a problem and you can't marshal the forces of good to help yourself or others be safer and more at peace.

One good way to determine whether evil is involved is how you feel around some people, and through the results of their actions. Do you feel afraid when around a particular person, or when involved with a group or place of employment? Do they say one thing but do another? Do things always go wrong around that person? Chances are evil is at work; not necessarily demons, but evil nonetheless. It's useful to know that no matter how profitable an agreement with evil souls—human or demon—might seem, you will always lose. As Mark Goulston says in his book, *Just Listen* (AMACOM, 2015), with some people, it doesn't matter how attractive the deal they offer you. Nothing good will ever come of it for you. Only the other person will benefit while you experience loss and distress. My advice? Walk away from evil souls, whether they are human or demons.

## *Mary, Queen of Scots harbored a demon*

When I became a practicing psychic, I gave away all psychic sessions for free. One of my first clients came from the same greater soul as Mary, Queen of Scots. (The client didn't tell me this; that's the information I received psychically when I worked with her.) When I started working with this client, I found a malevolent presence in her energy field.

It wasn't my first time encountering a demon, but it was my first time encountering a demon in the presence of a client. Although I'd been attacked by a powerful demon a few years before (the leader of a specific religious organization whose attention I caught when I resisted the efforts of some of that church's workers, people I call dark psychics; that is, psychics who attack and punish others who don't cave to the pressures from people in the religion), I hadn't yet learned how to deal with demons. I'd managed to bring that earlier encounter to a draw by following some half-understood advice from an online group I sought help from, and I never wanted another such encounter.

With this woman, I didn't know what the evil presence was. I was new to sharing my psychic abilities with others. I didn't know anything about dealing with that level of malevolence. All I knew was that it was bad energy, seemed sentient, and very much did not want to budge. It took me a long, terrifying time to remove the presence from that woman's energy field. (Kids, don't try this at home. I was lucky and I had powerful protection and divine help.)

A psychic colleague later told me that I'd been dealing with a demon, which was both scary and reassuring. Scary, because it was my first time experiencing that level of malevolence up close and personal (not counting my mother), and reassuring because I hadn't been harmed.

The next thing I'm going to say might surprise some folks. The presence I'd removed from that client's field was a demon who had tainted many related incarnated lifetimes of the woman I was helping, including Mary, Queen of Scots. My feeling was that Mary, Queen of Scots, initiated the contact with the demon, but I never investigated to find out for sure, nor do I want to. Not my circus, not my monkeys. Though it might explain why King James, Mary's son, introduced so many anti-witch injunctions into his translation of the Bible. (I say "his translation" because he commissioned it and, as king, had authority to dictate what he wanted in the translation. I say "introduced" because it has since been shown how much of the King James version of the Bible has material in it that never was in the original texts.)

After that psychic session, not because of the evil energy but because the woman was a taker and a leech, I told her I no longer wanted her to contact me. Unfortunately, the woman invited the demon back. I know this because I later saw her in a grocery store—her presence was chilling. Some people just like bad company.

## *Demons can be redeemed*

After that terrifying encounter, I didn't encounter another demon for some time. Along the way, I don't remember where or when, I'd gotten some new information and developed a new approach to dealing with demons. The next time I encountered a demon, I was calm and fearless, and I have remained so in the face of demons ever since. Now, instead of trying to wrestle with the demon and force them out of or away from someone, I speak with them with compassion. I give them a version of "the talk" (the talk I give souls who are possessing other people, or who haven't left their dead bodies—see chapter 13) tailored for their situation.

Here's how the demon-specific talk goes.

I tell them that in all my years as a psychic, I've learned that nothing 100% evil can exist. That's because evil carries within itself the seeds of its own destruction. If something were to somehow impossibly reach a state of 100% evil, it would vanish.

But nothing evil vanishes because everything, even the most evil being, has a spark of the divine in it. And furthermore, the divinity that created us all neither judges nor condemns anything created. We've all been given free will. Any choices we've made can be remade. Everyone who wishes to goes to heaven, but because of free will, no one is forced to go there. All this applies to demon kind as well.

If a demon wants to change, they can. And many are eager to once they hear my talk. This used to surprise me; I've dealt with psychopaths who are less open to grace than demons. Demons have to walk a long road back to the light and love of the divine, but they can do it. And that's generally where the demon-specific talk ends. Most of the demons I've given this talk to had persisted in being demons because they thought they were condemned forever for their choices. In for a penny, in for a pound, they thought, and they continued to be demony because they thought they had no other choice. Once they hear my talk, they recognize the truth in my words and they depart from whomever it is they're bothering. They often being to work their way back to the divine. As they do so, they'll reach a state where they'll be trusted enough to perform a sort of spiritual community service in which they become what a psychic friend calls the hunters.

The hunters help keep earthly neighborhoods clear of energetic garbage, the kind of psychic debris that people give off when they haven't learned that (a) they're generating and shedding this kind of energetic garbage, and therefore (b) they need to be more responsible about this kind of careless treatment of their surroundings.

The garbage also comes from other sources. The hunters don't deal with the sources; they just take care of keeping the streets clean of the energetic garbage.

By the time a demon has reached the stage of being a hunter, they are no longer what I call demons. Being a hunter shows they've reached a certain level of redemption. They're regaining their divine birthright and are therefore more distinctly good. (But still not human—as I said earlier, I don't think demon souls started as human souls, but instead are their own kind of being. In fact, the different types of hunters show me that the demons start out as different types of souls, sometimes including the other kinds of souls living in human bodies that I mentioned earlier.)

Eventually, after sufficient community service as a hunter, the former demons are promoted into another role. I haven't seen what the next role is, nor have I asked, but I know it's closer to the divine than the former demons had been in a long time.

## *The demon talk doesn't always work*

I once told a woman I would give her a psychic reading in exchange for her cleaning my house. (She didn't have money to pay for a reading, and she offered a house cleaning instead.) I don't remember how I met her—it might have been at an author's presentation at a local bookstore—but I do know at the time I was incautious and didn't set good boundaries in my life. She begged for help, and I agreed.

She showed up at my house for her reading, and I quickly realized she was full on possessed. During her reading, she barked; she sometimes spoke roughly and violently to me, often in a deeply masculine voice unlike her normal voice; she twisted her neck and held her head at angles that seemed nearly impossible.

Looking at the situation psychically, I saw that she was inhabited by hosts of demons. Hundreds of thousands of them. I'd never seen so many demons in one place before.

Somehow I was calm and unafraid.

I gave them the talk, and all but one of them cleared out immediately.

That one demon wasn't having it. He was the head of all those legions, and he liked being in control, and he wasn't pleased with me telling his legions they had free will and were redeemable.

He also didn't want to leave this woman.

I dug deeper, psychically speaking, and found a significant event in one of this woman's related lives, an event in which the woman's related self and this demon first connected and got entangled with each other. In that event, the related self made a mistake, got fearful and confused, and asked for help. The demon offered that help at the price of controlling her. She agreed, feeling she was safer with his strength. He then connected through time and space with many of her related selves and invaded them, including the one sitting in front of me, always with the same offer: "You aren't strong enough to survive life, so let me control you."

As I worked with her, I explained the circumstances of that decision and told the woman she didn't have to continue the agreement with the demon. I told her that he was only still there because she wanted him to be; that she was continuing to give him permission to control her because she didn't believe she was strong enough to survive without him. I explained that she was strong enough, and if she withdrew her permission, he couldn't stay. She accepted that she was being controlled by a demon and had been host to legions of other demons as well; that fact didn't surprise her at all.

Unfortunately, and to my astonishment, she refused to withdraw her permission to be possessed and controlled by the demon. She preferred having someone else to blame (the demon) for her choices and actions; she wasn't ready yet to start accepting responsibility for herself.

And because of her choice, I was unable to persuade the demon to leave. Unlike most demons who are demons because of bad choices and fear, yet who knew they had made bad choices and felt some guilt over their actions, he liked being bad. Some demons (and other souls) are like that. He felt no remorse for the harm he had caused and was continuing to cause. He wasn't going to leave unless she rejected him, and that wasn't happening.

The woman left my house still possessed by that one demon, who was worse than the legions of demons I had persuaded to leave her.

I don't know if any of the legions returned at the main demon's behest, but I suspect they wouldn't want to, having been shown hope, and didn't return. That doesn't mean the big bad didn't then draw in other legions. If he did, the woman wasn't going to oppose such an action.

After thinking about this experience for a few days, I called the woman and told her the reading was free; that I didn't want her to come clean my house as we'd agreed because I didn't want her leaving her demon-possessed energy all over my house. Yes, I was this blunt. She was understandably offended, but given a choice between offending someone and allowing them back into my house while they were still willingly saddled with a demon, I chose the former.

What do I mean when I say she would have been leaving her energy all over my house? Science teaches us that we are each made of atoms. Each atom is made of tiny particles, including particles called electrons. Electrons circle their atoms and sometimes jump around. When we touch something, some of the electrons in our atoms exchange themselves with some of the electrons in the thing we're touching.

Electrons are quantum particles and are subject to quantum entanglement. Quantum entanglement means that two electrons, once together, are in communication with each other no matter how distant they might become.

If I had let that woman clean my house, she would have been exchanging her demon-possessed electrons with everything she touched in my house. That's why I noped out of that situation.

As a side note, many psychics use an ability called psychometry, in which they touch an object once owned by someone and get information about that someone. I have a theory that the reason psychometry works is in part because of quantum entanglement. The person who owned the object exchanged some of their electrons with the object, and a talented psychic can read that person's energy and information from the electrons the person left in the object.

## *We have nothing to fear from demons*

By now it should be clear that you have nothing to fear from demons. They can only affect you if you give them permission. And even if you encounter one, you can give them my talk. That ought to get them moving in the right direction, which is away from you and toward the divine.

If you do encounter one of the tougher sort of demons, or find that your fear prevents you from holding compassion in your heart for the demon, seek help from a competent psychic or priest who is open to the existence of demons.

Before you do, though, know that not all experiences that look like possession are possession. They can be explained by and treated as psychological or physical events, and a good counselor or physician can help resolve the apparent possession.

Therefore, if you think you or someone you know is possessed by a demon, the first step is to eliminate the possibility that it's psychological or physical (something not working properly in your brain or body, for example) and then, if needed, to exorcise the possessing being. As Father Amorth said, it can hurt nothing to hold an exorcism. You'll need both a counselor and a priest (and maybe a good psychic, though there can be antipathy between the three professions) to help you sort it out.

An exorcist will take a different approach than I do. Exorcists see exorcism as a fight and see demons as irredeemable and eternally damned; beings that must be wrestled with and cast out with threats. Nonetheless, exorcisms can work. And maybe it's the only way for those demons who enjoy being a demon, such as the one possessing the woman I just spoke of.

One reason I've spent time talking about demons is to show that **if even demons are redeemable, then you are too**. You may think you aren't redeemable; maybe you've done things no human soul can forgive. But don't give up on yourself. The Divine never has and never will. If the Divine can forgive even demons, then you are also forgivable and redeemable. The Divine is vast, vaster than our universe, and is infinitely capable of forgiveness and mercy.

# Chapter 8
# A new theory of reincarnation

Often my clients ask about lives they lived as the same soul but in another body, place, and time. They see it as asking about past lives. I see it as the client needing information from another aspect of the greater soul they are a part of. In the end, it doesn't matter. What's important is that a client gets good results from the work I do with souls that are connected to them in some way. In the rest of this chapter, I talk about linear time and reincarnation from a new perspective, one that I've never seen anyone else present.

## *Concepts of time*

First, let's talk about time. Like many people, I, too, once believed in the conventional ideas of linear time and reincarnation, and was in touch with what I used to think were my past and future lives. With one difference: Based on my ability to communicate with beings anywhere in any time, I came to believe that all events and times are simultaneous, so I believed at the time that that although we as the same soul incarnated in various times and places, those incarnations were simultaneous.

Because of that belief in simultaneity, I believed that, although it wasn't meaningless to talk of past or future lives, I didn't think it useful to think in those terms. During a psychic reading, if I was so guided, I would tune into what I thought were a person's other lifetimes, trusting that the information I received was relevant to my client's present time. I would explain to my clients that all time is simultaneous, so all our lives are happening now, communicating with and affecting other lives at the same time, and that anything happening in those other lives was affecting the client's present life, and vice versa. Here's an analogy of what I mean.

Imagine all times are countries on earth..Just as the different countries exist at the same time, but in different places, all times exist at the same time, just in different "zones." So, for example, CE 1899 is in one "time continent," CE 1924 is in another "time continent/zone," and BCE 3500 is in a third. Just like with people living on different continents, where you can use a telephone to call someone in another country, that's how I see people in other times. They all exist in the eternal Now. People are alive in their own times, and I, as a spirit communication specialist who can communicate with anyone, anywhere, in any time and place, can use my psychic telephone to "call" people in their here and now from my here and now. Therefore the word "past" is only meaningful when talking about time as a linear phenomenon.

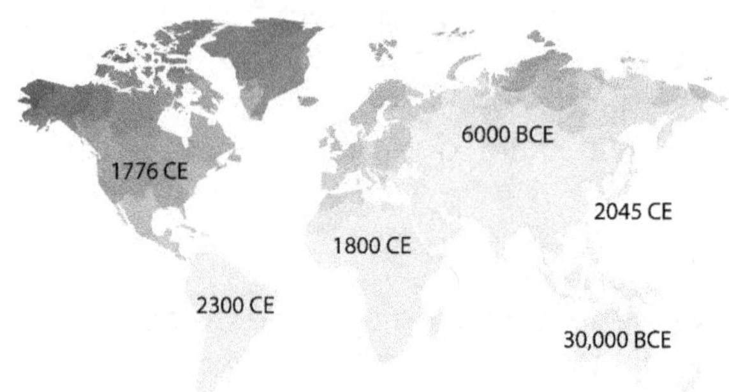


*Figure 21. Because time is simultaneous, just as we can telephone anyone on earth, we can psychically communicate with anyone anywhere in any time.*

## *Traditional beliefs about reincarnation*

Reincarnation is the belief that we, the same soul that we are now, return to life again and again. The core idea is that our essence—some call it a soul, some call it a flame, some call it other things—lives many lifetimes, returning many times to physical existence in some form or another, usually in a linear time fashion. Although the belief may have been around longer, scholars say people have believed in reincarnation for about 2,500 years, and some Biblical scholars point to places in the Bible that seem to indicate the Bible's writers believed in reincarnation.

You'll find many variations on this belief in reincarnation.

Some people believe we only reincarnate some set number of years after our bodily death, or we only reincarnate in a human body, or we only reincarnate if we were bad in our previous life and must atone for our badness in a new life. Some believe we can only be in one body at a time—that it isn't possible to live more than one life simultaneously with another. Others believe that it's possible for the same soul to live overlapping lives, because souls aren't limited by time and space.

Some believe we return in many types of bodies—human, cat, dog, salmon, and so on. The Welsh poet Taliesin Henwg (534-599 CE) wrote "The Battle of Goddeu" (also known as "The Battle of the Trees"), a poem whose topics include life, existence, and reincarnation. Others believe only human souls can incarnate in human bodies, and that other types of souls incarnate in other types of bodies—cat souls incarnate in cat bodies, dog souls incarnate in dog bodies, and so on.

Some believe that what you reincarnate as is a result of what you did in a previous life. If we did bad things in a previous life, we are punished somehow in this life by being placed in bad circumstances or in an insect's body and so on.

When I believed in reincarnation, I believed what many who believe in reincarnation believe: That decisions we make in another life affected decisions we make now, regardless of when that other lifetime is playing out. During a psychic reading, I often communicated with a person's other selves living in another time where that other self's decisions were affecting my client's here and now, and had in many cases been affecting that client their entire life. That other self made a bad decision whose effects rippled out to other lifetimes, causing those other lifetimes difficulties.

To fix or at least ameliorate the bad effects, I would contact my client's other self in that other self's life at some time before the bad decision and give them information from a higher perspective, more information than they had available to them. Then that other self could make a different decision when they reached that decision point in their lives. By giving them that information, and because time is simultaneous, I helped those other selves change their own futures as well as the lives of the other affected selves. In this way, in a single psychic session, I've often helped clients resolve issues they'd suffered their entire lives.

When I've explained time this way, most people have found the idea of non-linear time easy to accept, even comfortable, and it helped them accept that the changes their other selves made in other times could affect them in the here and now.

### *What I now believe about reincarnation*

As I gained more experience as a psychic, and especially when talking with people in the afterlife, I started to wonder: If reincarnation is true, then why was I seeing all these dearly departed folks in the afterlife, including people's ancestors who lived long ago, and including people who were famous in their times? Why aren't they reincarnated? If time is simultaneous, why would we be punished by actions we are taking in another life at the same time as the life we're living now? If our souls can change their future in other lives, why do we suffer from the decisions we made in another life before we changed our future in that life?

The answers started coming to me in flashes of insight and observation, and with that new information, my beliefs about reincarnation have evolved. I went from believing that we come back repeatedly as the same soul in a new body, to the belief I hold today. Everything I now believe about reincarnation is based on my experiences as a psychic and on my interpretation of those experiences, plus information I've received from the spirit realm.

The most important part of my beliefs about reincarnation, about which I go into detail later in this chapter, is that there is and will only ever be one version of us as we are now here on earth. We as the soul that we are have never been here before and we will never be here again. Instead, we are each unique aspects of a greater soul that exists in and outside space and time. That greater soul, which some call our oversoul or our higher self, chooses to send aspects of itself into physical reality to incarnate in various times and places for many purposes. Just as we as a person have different moods and aspects, just so our greater soul or oversoul has different aspects, each of which can incarnate as a soul in physical reality. And there isn't one greater soul; instead, each of us has our own greater soul, and there are many greater souls.

Those aspects of our greater soul can come into physical reality in human bodies, and also in other types of bodies (cats, dogs, cockroaches....). Each of those aspects is unique; none ever repeats. The you that you are now in this time and place has never been on this earth before, nor will you ever be on this earth again. Although it isn't an exact analogy, one way to look at it is that each of us is an avatar of our greater soul. There is no such thing as a past life or future life or us living another life on earth; we just have this one go-round and then we're offski to other places.

I used to think of lifetimes that I remembered as past or future lives. Now, although I still have those memories, I know that those memories aren't mine, but instead are of other aspects of my greater soul that have incarnated. They are brother and sister selves, with whom I communicate and from whom I can learn, but they are not me, nor am I them. Although those other selves and I are each an aspect of our shared greater self, we are individual souls, not one soul. I call these other aspects "related selves." I can't claim to be important because of who any of my related selves are and what those related selves are doing in their lifetimes any more than they can claim to be important because of who I am and what I am doing. The only way in which our related selves are one soul is in our shared existence as facets (or aspects or avatars) of our greater self.

Kind of a bummer for the ego, no? Yet also freeing and a relief. We didn't do those bad things our related selves have done in their lifetimes, yet we can learn from them. Nor can we claim credit for the wonderful things those other selves are doing in their lifetimes, though we can benefit from them.

I now know that when I thought I was communicating with a client's "past" lives, I was instead communicating with one of the client's related selves, a self whose decisions were affecting the client and the client's other related selves. (Later in this chapter, I explain in more detail how this works.) In a sense it doesn't matter whether those were past lives or relates selves: The results for my clients were the same: Their lives improved because of the changes their related selves made because of the new information I brought them.

From one perspective, you *are* those other souls that are part of your greater soul, and they are you. From that perspective, you can incorporate this new idea while continuing to believe in past/future lives.

As a side note, when I still believed that I was a single soul that reincarnated, I noticed that all my incarnations that I was aware of had strong physical resemblances to each other, regardless of whether they were male or female. (Regarding incarnations that were famous, or infamous, enough to have been painted or photographed.) I now think the resemblance is a marker of the greater soul. Or it could be a shared characteristic of related souls that are closer to each other in terms of common themes we're working on.

## *Our relationship with our greater soul*

You might think that everyone would want the help and guidance their greater souls can offer; after all, our greater selves exist both inside and outside of time and space, and can guide us with a lot of information and advice we might not otherwise receive. But that's not always the case.

Some people have so completely rejected their greater selves that they ignore all communications from their greater selves. They also can't learn from their related selves. One time a client had so thoroughly rejected everything having to do with a greater existence that they refused to accept messages, information, and help from their greater self, let alone from related selves. The image I saw was of my client as a soul with their back turned to their greater self, arms crossed, face with a stubbornly mulish expression. That person was so entrenched in their rejection that their greater self could do nothing but honor that person's free will.

My client's greater self had stopped trying to get through to that person, though they, the greater self, was quite willing to speak with me in yet another effort to get through to my client. (Since my client had come to me for psychic information, their greater self chose to interpret that as my client being open to the idea of reconnecting.) My client's greater self wanted to resume communications as soon as my client was willing to stop refusing the connection. When I told my client this, they reiterated their absolute rejection of any such connection, and, as I looked at my client's most probable futures, it looked as though my client wasn't going to change. Maybe they chose the path of rejecting spiritual guidance so they could learn what it was like to completely cut themselves off from any kind of spiritual help.

Eventually they'll reconnect, though that may happen after they leave their body. Maybe that reconnection will be a shock, maybe it will be a relief. Either way, it's not my business to know.

## *How I came to believe in reincarnation and how those beliefs evolved*

In the late 1970s, for an entire year, I had a series of dreams of a life lived in the American Old West. In those dreams, I was an adventurous journalist, writer, and lover of cats, and I spent a lot of time in California. Each dream was a different detailed adventure; sometimes I was in San Francisco, and sometimes in what is now Tuolumne County, California, where gold and silver mining was making many folks rich. In many of these dreams, I had the same friend. When I woke from the dreams that included the friend, I thought the friend felt like Pete, one of my brothers in this life.

Eventually I had the courage to tell Pete my dreams. He surprised me by saying he'd been having similar dreams. Only in his dreams, his friend felt to him like it was me.

I decided that we were remembering past lifetimes we had shared, and I went with that belief for many years. After that year, I started to remember what I thought at the time were many other lifetimes, some of interesting, even holy, people, and some unholy. I believed those memories were of me, the same soul, experiencing different lives.

My understanding of and beliefs in reincarnation stayed the same for many years: that a single soul would be reborn again and again in different bodies in a linear fashion throughout time.

Then in the 1980s, after I admitted to myself that I was psychic and had been my entire life, and started acknowledging information received through those senses, my understanding of reincarnation began to evolve.

Most of my life I've felt drawn to the image of the Tree of Life —the one that shows birds in a tree, representing the Tree of Life described in the book of Genesis in the Hebrew Bible (which Christians call the Old Testament). For those unfamiliar with the story, next to the Tree of Life in the Garden of Eden stood the tree of knowledge of good and evil, which was a tree of duality— a tree God pointed to and forbade Adam and Eve from eating its fruits. As we all know, that restriction didn't go well and Adam and Eve ignored God's injunction. Setting aside what I think of the tree of duality, I've long felt the tree of life image was a rich and deeply layered symbol, and, as I said, I was strongly drawn to it, but I had no clue what it might mean.

Then one day a few decades ago, when my questions about reincarnation were growing based on the contradictions I was seeing, both psychically and logically, in beliefs about classical reincarnation, I was reading Ferrar Fenton's translation of the Bible for the first time. Ferrar Fenton (1832-1920) was born into a family with generations of multilingual people, and he shared the family talents. He spoke 25 languages and dialects. He once said his family was used to making multilingual jokes, an impressive fact. It's hard enough to be humorous in just one language.

Although Fenton worked as a businessman to pay the bills, his life work was spending fifty years translating the Bible. Contrary to common practice, he didn't rely on other people's translations, but instead translated from original texts as much as possible—Greek and Hebrew texts chief among them. Scandalously for his Christian social milieu, he consulted with Jewish scholars on the finer points of the meanings of Hebrew words and phrases. How very dare.

In his introduction to his translation, Fenton said that he was surprised at the many things that are in other translations that weren't in the source materials, and conversely, he was surprised at the many things in the original texts that aren't in the traditional translations (that is, original text had been removed from the translations). Further, he said, he translated many things differently than was traditional. He said there were too many such differences to list, and left it to his readers to find those differences.

One of the things I noticed immediately in Fenton's translation is that he translated the phrase "Tree of Life" as "Tree of Lives," plural. Here's the text:

"And out of the ground the EVER-LIVING GOD caused to grow all the trees that were beautiful and good for food, as well as the Tree of Lives in the center of the Garden; and the tree of the Knowledge of Good and Evil."

A light ignited in my brain, and I got a new vision of reincarnation that reconciled many of the inconsistencies that had bothered me between what I believed about reincarnation and what I had seen as a psychic. I suddenly saw the tree of life as a symbol for our soul's existence in and outside space and time.

## *The Tree of Life is about reincarnation*

As I say earlier in this chapter, most people speaking of reincarnation speak of past lives and sometimes future lives. Yet thinking in terms of past and future is only a construct we use to understand time. As I said earlier, I see all time as simultaneous.

As I've learned from Metatron and Seth and my other nonphysical teachers, and as I also came to believe because of my inspiration gained from learning that the Tree of Life should be called the Tree of Lives, each of us is a unique facet of a greater soul that exists outside space and time. That doesn't mean there is one vast amorphous soul that exists everywhere and at all times that all of us are a part of. Instead, it means that many greater souls exist outside space and time. Most of those greater souls wish to experience life in time and space. (I'll call this 4D life, for four-dimensional life; I also refer to it as physical reality, which is made of three physical dimensions and time, the fourth dimension.) To do so, a greater soul inserts facets of itself into the space-time continuum—not just one facet over and over again, but many facets, each living in 4D reality only once.

## *We are each facets of our greater souls*

What do I mean by "facets"? Just as each of us humans have different moods and ways of expressing ourselves, the greater soul that we are part of has different aspects. The greater soul is far greater, far more varied, and far more complex than we are. (And we humans are pretty complex creatures, but the principle is the same. As it is above, so it is below.) Each of those facets is a unique expression of that greater soul and will never be duplicated. Each facet has many purposes, things they are in physical reality to accomplish. Our greater soul assigns those purposes before sending us, an aspect or facet of itself, into physical reality. Some facets share similar purposes, some are working on something completely different. And many of those facets are incarnated as individuals on this planet, somewhere and some-when in time. All those facets live, grow, and die within the matrix of time and space, doing its best to understand and accomplish its purposes. Each decision each of those facets makes affects some or all other facets—sometimes strongly, sometimes not at all, depending on what each facet's purposes are and how closely the facet follows the will of the greater soul, a will the facet agreed with before it incarnated, but which it can diverge from because of free will..

We aren't all part of one greater soul. Instead, many greater souls exist, each with its set of aspects that it sends into physical reality to live and learn. That means I am an aspect of my greater soul and you are an aspect of your greater soul. It's possible that two people can be aspects of the same greater soul, and sometimes we sense that truth when we meet other related selves from our specific greater soul. But we aren't all part of only one greater soul.

As an aside, in all my decades of being a practicing psychic, I've never seen anything resembling twin flames—souls that are two halves of the same soul, one each in a separate physical body. People who promote the idea of twin flames say you must be in a relationship with your twin flame, or your life is incomplete. I have seen related souls existing in the same milieu, but that's not the same as one soul split into two parts and incarnating in separate bodies. Our related souls are each whole, while also being a part of a greater soul, and are not tied inextricably to each other or fated to be together. Because I have never seen split or divided souls, I believe the twin flames idea is a misunderstanding and is susceptible to being abused and misused. However, it's possible that I simply haven't seen a split soul—after all, reality is wide and complex and perhaps I just haven't encountered that specific phenomenon. Though I doubt it. The idea simply doesn't make sense in light of what I've seen and understand.

On the other hand, it's possible for more than one soul to share the same body, usually in cases of possession, but not always. I talk about possession in chapter 13.

### *Our related souls in the afterlife*

When we or our related selves leave our physical bodies, we go to the afterlife, where we reconnect more consciously with our greater soul. We as a facet of our greater soul aren't destroyed, nor are we absorbed back into the greater self. Instead, in the afterlife, we continue as our unique selves, living and learning about reality, and we continue learning how to be better beings—more caring, more responsible, more compassionate. We are still a part of our greater self, and we are still in communication with both our greater selves and, if we want to be, with our related selves. We continue to work on our purposes, which expand with our expanded reality. Eventually we evolve and become more integrated with our related selves and our greater selves, to the point where we are each aware of our individual existence, yet we also know we are part of a greater whole.

Eventually, after evolving through space and time, all the facets start thinking of themselves as part of the great collective that is their greater self, and at that point, they start thinking and communicating in terms of "we." When Metatron speaks with me, he often uses "we" when speaking of himself, and so I believe that he, too, evolved as a greater soul's set of related selves until he arrived at his present position of being in charge of the entirety of physical existence.

## *Each facet of a greater soul affects all other facets to some extent*

How does this idea of us each being a facet of a greater soul work in practical terms? When some other facet of your greater soul—let's call that other facet Robin—makes a decision in their time, that decision reverberates through the fabric of space and time, and into the greater soul of which each facet is a part. Those decisions also affect all other facets of our greater soul to a greater or lesser extent. Because all time is simultaneous, there is no such thing as a past life (or a future one, for that matter). Therefore, Robin's decisions affect you regardless of when in time Robin exists.

However, how much Robin's decisions affect you depends on how closely you each are exploring the same aspects of life. Let's say Robin is exploring and learning about the same kinds of things you are. In that case, Robin's decisions affect you more strongly than they affect another facet of your greater soul that might be exploring other aspects of life and reality.

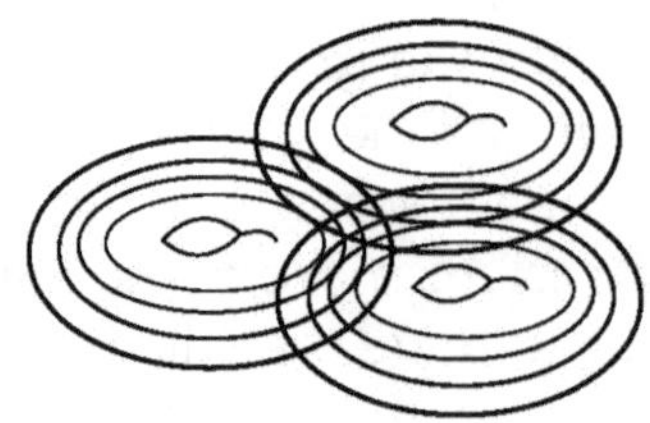

*Figure 22. Decisions a soul makes in its lifetime ripple out from that lifetime and affect related souls that are working on similar concerns in other lifetimes. When we change ourselves, we affect our related selves, and vice versa.*

When I do readings with people and access their other lifetimes, the lifetimes I see most prominently are those in which a facet of that person's greater soul is making a decision that is affecting the person I am doing the reading for. I give that other facet enough information to make a different decision, and that change affects the person I am doing the reading with. I see those other facets, those related souls, as part of the specific multidimensional soul (the greater soul) that the client is a part of. When a client needs me to, I communicate with their relevant related soul facets.

Let's use the Tree of Life as an analogy.

## *The Tree of Life illustrates our existence in and outside of space and time*

The Tree of Life is an excellent analogy for our existence in and outside space and time. Think of the tree's trunk as our greater soul. The tree's branches and twigs represent our greater soul reaching into various realities, including physical reality. Many greater souls exist, each its own tree, but for simplicity, I'm only talking about one greater soul (represented as one tree) and its facets.

The leaves on the branches and twigs represent individual facets of the greater soul. Each leaf is unique and represents a single life lived in a specific reality. Leaves on a particular twig and branch are "closer" to each other in terms of similarities and interests of the greater soul, and therefore more strongly affect each other. A specific branch and its collection of leaves are focused on one set of questions; another branch and its collection of leaves are focused on another set of questions. Just as anything significant happening to us affects our nearby related facets, anything significant happening to a nearby facet (another leaf on the same branch or twig) affects us more strongly than events happening on more distant branches.

The birds on the Tree of Life represent messages passing among the individual lives, making it possible to receive messages swiftly and directly from any other leaf on the tree. I believe the bird messengers represent communications from our greater self (the tree), and also represent our related selves sending messages directly to each other.

*Figure 23. A Tree of Life. The trunk and branches represent our greater self that gives birth to, holds, and nurtures each leaf, which is an individual soul. Each soul is an aspect of our greater self, incarnating on earth. Leaves on the same branch or twig represent souls working on similar questions assigned by our greater self. Leaves (related selves) on further-away branches or twigs are working on other questions. Our greater self exists inside and outside of space and time.*

When our bodies die, we as a soul move on to the afterlife as the same soul we were in life, and then from there to other adventures. We are still a part of our greater soul, still communicating with that greater soul, yet we remain individual souls. What was created will never be destroyed, by which I mean we don't vanish into nothingness. Eventually, after many adventures as a soul, we reintegrate into our greater soul, yet still remain distinct and distinctly aware of ourselves within that greater self.

While living on the physical earth, when we "remember" what we think of as another lifetime, we aren't remembering something we, the soul living this life now, did in another life. That's impossible. We as the soul we are will never return in a body to this planet again. Instead, with those memories, we are accessing the memories of a related facet of our greater self. That related facet isn't the same soul as we are. But because that facet is a part of our greater soul, those memories feel like our own. And from that perspective, because those other facets are not us but are related to us, it makes sense that our related selves can live lives that overlap with the lives of other related selves.

Yet just because those memories aren't our own doesn't mean they aren't useful. We can learn from our related facets' experiences, just as they can learn from ours, especially if those other souls are working on similar questions.

## *Changing decisions in related lives can help this life*

I do what I used to call past-life healing sessions. I now see them as sessions in which I bring information to a client's related self so that related self can make different decisions and therefore change and heal themselves. And although my view on reincarnation has changed over the years, that kind of session is still as useful and powerful as it has ever been.

When in the past I thought I was healing other lifetimes, I was instead helping related souls heal themselves, and the changes arising out of their self-healing affected my clients in this life. Those sessions are powerfully effective regardless of what I believe the healing mechanism is. Usually it only takes one session to clear up a lifelong pattern my client has had.

When I say "healing," I don't mean *I* do the healing. Nobody heals anybody else. Instead, someone who can be thought of as a healer is instead a facilitator: They make available to their clients the information and energies the client needs to accomplish their own healing. I have been told numerous times by other psychics that I am a natural healer. Those other psychics explained that because of who I am, I was actively healing people without doing anything consciously.

Back then, I believed those psychics. Now, I have a somewhat more nuanced view: I believe that yes, by just being in my presence, without me doing anything, people are being healed, but I'm not doing the healing. Instead, people in my presence are exposed through me to spiritual energies that open the door to their greater reality, making it possible for them to manage their own healing processes. This is what those many psychics meant when they said I am a natural healer.

I've developed this belief for three reasons. The first is I believe we heal ourselves. The second is because of what I've experienced in my psychic readings that has led me to believe that we are each in charge of ourselves. During a psychic reading, I am at a more expanded level of awareness and am accessing information and making available energies from our greater reality. (In my mind, information = energy.) My client, the person I am psychically accessing information for, joins me on that expanded level of awareness and is immersed in those energies. When I ask during the reading if they have questions, they often say "no, everything is clear" because they are on that level and are bathed in those energies. In that moment, they know and understand more than they normally would.

Later, when they are back to their usual level of consciousness and awareness, they have questions, or ask me to remind them of what I said. This is because once the reading ended, they stopped being in that state of expanded awareness and stopped having access to the information I was making available. This is why I recommend to my clients that they allow me to record the session so they can listen to it later. The same energies that were present during the reading are present in the recording. In case you're wondering, I never record a reading without permission. I also never keep those recordings unless something universally useful was said in the reading, in which case I ask permission to keep that portion of the reading, scrubbed of all identifying information. Consent and permission are paramount.

Likewise, the same energies I imbue in everything I do, including my psychic sessions, are also present in my writings, including this book.

The third reason is that many years ago, the entity Seth gave a message about healing (https://thelighthouseonline.com/channel/Seth_on_energy.html) in which he said, in part, "Your role as a healer is to, you might say, with one hand reach into the universal love energy, and with the other reach into the individual's energy, and connect them. It is your job as a healer to understand and tune into, as much as possible, the individual energy of the person you are working with, connect them with the healing love energy in such a way that their individuality is enhanced and nurtured and made more able to express its own uniqueness. ... [Y]ou are seeking to bring that love energy into them so that they can use it however they like. They can customize it, if you will; they can make it their own and have it express their own unique talents, abilities, and selfness, selfhood."

If asked, I will send healing energies to others, but I only do that when asked; I never send such energies without permission, and I don't actively apply those healing energies to the other person. Instead, I make those energies available to others to use as they wish. More usually, rather than sending healing energies, I ask for help on their behalf: I ask that the person be able to see the help and healing energies they are surrounded with. That help and those energies are in the other person's hands to use as they wish. I consider this approach to be the most respectful of a person's free will. I suppose you could consider this kind of request as a form of prayer, and I'm okay with that. Prayer in whatever form is powerful and is always listened to.

## *Time is simultaneous*

I mentioned earlier that we tend to experience time as a linear flow from past to present to future.

In my experience as a psychic, another way to view and experience time is as being simultaneous. I say this because I often communicate with people in other times, and to them, they are still alive. Not only that, as I've discussed, I've often helped people change their lives in their personal now by helping a related facet of their greater soul change the related facet's life "then," in what we perceive of as the past.

Let me explain. But first, a caveat.

## *Before blaming other lives, look at this life first*

If you believe in reincarnation in the usual model (that one soul lives many lifetimes), it can be tempting to blame a previous lifetime for difficulties you're experiencing now. It's a way to say, "Sorry, not sorry," because you believe you're a victim of a previous self or of a punishing God, and can't do anything about your life now because of that previous lifetime. It can be easier to say "It's their fault" than to accept responsibility for your choices in this life (or any other life). Yet I encourage you to think differently and more responsibly about such things. Blaming anyone else is denying your power in the present. Jane Roberts brought through a message from the entity Seth saying (in an unpublished ESP class held February 5, 1974), "You are not powerless before your past...you are born anew in this moment. Therefore...use it to assert the independence and the joy and the vitality of your being. From here, you make your reality, not from the past."

Since you already know what I think about the importance of responsibility, I won't talk about that aspect. Instead, whether you believe in classical reincarnation or accept this new perspective, it's not useful to blame other lives or your related selves for the pickle you're in in this life.

Although your related selves' decisions and actions can *affect* you, those selves aren't to blame for your experiences now. Let's say you are suffering from a pattern of life experiences that can't be explained by your earlier experiences in this life. In such cases, many people who believe in reincarnation decide to abdicate all responsibility for themselves and instead blame other lifetimes, saying they are suffering from bad karma (or whatever they choose to call it) because of decisions they made in another life.

But blaming another life for problems you're having in this life takes away your agency and your ability to fix those problems. Even within the reincarnation/karma model, it's still your responsibility to work on whatever needs fixing in this life. So check this life first before blaming a related self for your experiences. Instead of being a victim of a previous life, maybe you are suffering from the effects of unrecognized, unacknowledged, and untreated childhood trauma in this lifetime; or from unrecognized, undiagnosed, and untreated attention deficit disorder (ADD), which can lead to anxiety and depression; or any of a host of issues arising from decisions and life circumstances in the here and now that you can take charge of. (I believe that many more of us than are aware experienced childhood trauma and adverse childhood events. Once we realize we experienced those things, we can start healing ourselves of those effects.)

To get closer to a solution, learn as much as you can about yourself and your life before pointing a finger at a related life. Read books and articles. See a counselor or faith leader. If you don't get along with the first counselor or faith leader you consult, don't give up on the whole profession. Counselors and faith leaders are people, not machines. They vary in their skills and in their personalities. You might come across a counselor or faith leader who just isn't compatible with you, or who lacks the skills and knowledge needed to help you. You might even come across an unethical counselor who will mess with you to keep you as a client. I once knew a woman who had been seeing the same counselor for ten years. She hadn't improved as a human being in any way; in fact, she got worse. (I knew her throughout those years.) Yet the counselor kept dangling the carrot of recovery in front of her, and she, oblivious and un-self-aware, kept pursuing that never-delivered carrot. *Caveat emptor* (a Latin phrase meaning "let the buyer beware").

## *How helping a related soul can help our problems in this life*

Let's say you can't pinpoint anything in this life that could be a root cause for something troubling you in the here and now. After you've honestly examined all possibilities, you decide to look into other, related lifetimes. You may still have causes from this lifetime, but in such cases, it can be helpful to look into related lifetimes as well.

Again, in my experience, none of us ever live another life. Instead, other facets of our greater self are living other lives, and we in this life are connected to those other facets, those related souls, some more closely than others.

Let's say you come to me, your psychic, seeking insight into a persistent feeling that you are unworthy somehow—that somehow, somewhere, you made a terrible mistake and deserve to be punished for it, and so every time something is going well for you, you manage to sabotage it.

Many people have this feeling because they were the scapegoat of a narcissistic parent or otherwise had terrible family experiences as a child. If that's you, you have my deep compassion and sympathy. What you went through was horrific. It's terrible to live with the constant sense of dread and terror of being a scapegoat or otherwise being traumatized; to never have felt safe, ever; to have only memories of the murderous rage in your mother or father's eyes as they screamed at you in private, then acted like a saint in public.

If that was your experience, I recommend learning about narcissism and people incapable of empathy. Read books and articles, watch YouTube videos ("Dr. Ramani" and "Surviving Narcissism" are two excellent sources of compassionate, gentle information on narcissism), talk with friends (though make sure they are truly your friends), and consult with a counselor or faith leader.

But make sure that counselor or faith leader is an expert in your specific type of circumstances. Many counselors have yet to learn enough about narcissism to be helpful, and some even still believe that the parent is always right and if a child complains about a parent, the child is lying. If you suspect you were the scapegoat of one or more narcissistic parents, it's hard to find a counselor or faith leader who understands narcissism, and who can help you. If you were the family scapegoat, read Jay Reid's 2023 book, *Growing Up as the Scapegoat to a Narcissistic Parent*. It's the clearest description of what life is like for the scapegoat that I have yet found anywhere.

If you don't have any experiences in this life that you can point to as the source for that something that is bugging you, at that point it can be helpful to look into the lifetimes of related souls to see if a related soul is making some decisions that are affecting you (and probably other related souls). You can do this yourself, but a skilled psychic can be quite helpful, especially in terms of bringing clarity and objectivity.

## *Healing yourself*

Let's say in your self-explorations you have some dreams, or intuitions, or otherwise receive information that a facet of your greater self (that is, a related soul) does indeed make a terrible mistake, one that can't be undone in the normal way. The horror and guilt from that related soul's lifetime is rippling out to and affecting the lives of other "close" related souls. By "close," I mean lives in which your greater soul is running similar life scenarios with several souls to learn something about a particular aspect of human experience. In the Tree of Life analogy, these lives are closest to each other on the same branches or twigs of the tree.

*Figure 24. How helping a related soul in their life can help you in this life.*

Even though it's not you but another related soul making that mistake, you can work with the related self to resolve the issue.

Because time is simultaneous, when I work with clients on other, related facets of their greater selves like this, I can bring to that other related self the information they need *before* they make the irrevocable mistake. If they choose to listen (and most do), they can make a different choice and avoid making the mistake.

In my experience, most other related souls can change their decisions in this way, changing their future, and by changing their future, they help their related selves (because they are no longer taking the action that caused the problem in the first place). Most of my clients only need one session to resolve a particular related soul's key issue.

But not always. A few times I haven't been able to help someone's related soul, though I was able to get enough information for that other related soul and my client to bring some spiritual relief to both. Sometimes, I suspect, a client is holding onto an issue because they aren't ready to accept responsibility for themselves, much as that possessed woman I spoke of in chapter 7 didn't want to refuse permission to the demon possessing her. For people not willing to accept responsibility, it's easier and more convenient to blame a related soul. For the few times when a client seemed ready to accept responsibility, though, I remain puzzled about why I haven't always been able to help completely. The only conclusion I have made so far is that the issue has deeper and wider ramifications that are too complicated to work on in one session, or that simply need to be that way for reasons I can't access.

## *How and why other selves affect us*

One time a group of psychics, including me, were socializing at a fellow psychic's house in Half Moon Bay, California. One of the psychics present, whom I will call Sura (not her real name), had made a name for herself in the South San Francisco Bay Area as a trance channeler.

Sura asked everyone present a favor. She said she wanted to be conscious when channeling, but had never been able to do so, and she didn't know why. Furthermore, she would often get terrible headaches after channeling. Could we look into it psychically to give her insight?

I listened as one psychic after another proposed their theory. It didn't seem that any of them was getting their information psychically, but they were instead hypothesizing based on what they thought the cause *could* be. Nothing wrong with that; rational thought is important! But after each statement, Sura politely said she didn't think that was the reason.

Finally, when it was my turn, I looked into the issue psychically and saw the details of a related soul. At the time I spoke of it as one of Sura's past lives, but now I would say it was the life of one of her related selves. I described what I saw happening and how the person in that life made some decisions based on their experiences. I explained how what I was seeing was related to Sura's experience. I also talked with that related self and gave him information he hadn't had before so he could make a different choice.

The next time I saw Sura, she told me that the first time she channeled after that meeting, she was conscious during the channeling, which she never had been before. She also said she never again had a headache after channeling. She attributed those changes to the information I'd given her. But, she said, it was too weird to be present and conscious in her body while someone else was using it, so she chose to not be conscious after all. It wasn't that I healed her; it was that I brought to her and her related self the information they both needed to heal themselves.

The takeaway here is that things we do and decisions our related selves make in other lives can affect us in this life, and if we can access that information, we can reduce or eliminate the effect those other lifetime decisions are having on us.

## *My skills as a natural psychic*

One possible reason for my being able to pinpoint Sura's problem when the other psychics couldn't is that I'm a natural psychic—I have never taken any kind of training to learn how to be psychic and have instead been taught by various spirits and divine beings. All the other psychics at this meeting had attended a popular San Francisco Bay Area school where they had been taught to be psychic. Awakening your psychic abilities through a formal school works, but I had finely tuned abilities that got better with time and practice and hadn't been limited by being told what was and wasn't possible for psychics to do. (One of the psychics who had attended the school told me she had never seen anyone communicate with spirits the way I did, and that furthermore, she'd been taught it was bad to communicate with spirits.) And in terms of time and psychic skills and experiences, I was far ahead of those other psychics, most of whom had only been practicing for a short while.

Just as with any other skill, the more you practice, the more you improve. John Muir Laws, a scientist and artist, often talks about "pencil miles"; he says that the more you draw, the better an artist you become. You just need to put in those pencil miles. The same is true for using your psychic abilities; as Metatron told me when I first started to communicate with him, the more you bring through the energies of communicating with other beings, the greater your ability grows to bring in even more and stronger energies. The analogy he gave me was that of a tiny channel in the dust: The channel can only carry so much water, but as the water flows through that channel, it widens and deepens the channel, making it more capable of carrying more water. Eventually you have the Grand Canyon, capable of carrying an enormous amount of water. Or, in the case of a psychic, an enormous amount of spiritual energy and information.

## *Our future related lives are also accessible*

When I first started to remember other lifetimes, I experienced them in full sight, sound, and color. In terms of time, some were from what we call the past from the perspective of time as a linear flow; others were from what we call the future.

When I first "remembered" a future life, I was dismayed. Not at the life itself—it ended rather heroically, with me saving a group of school children from the collapsing walls of a large building excavation in South America. That wasn't what dismayed me. At that time I believed in reincarnation as most people understand it, and believed in linear time, so I thought remembering a future life meant I was going to continue the reincarnational cycle. Yet somehow the actions I took and decisions I made in that life affected me in this one.

Later, as I had more experiences communicating with folks in other times and places, folks who to themselves were very much alive in their "present" (their times), I came to see time as simultaneous, not linear. I saw this even more when I remembered living three lifetimes simultaneously, not just in one era, but in a few. (I say "I," but I mean other close, related aspects of the greater soul we all share. But that's a mouthful, so I say "I" for short.)

*Figure 25. Time is simultaneous. All our related selves are alive now.*

For example, I know of three related selves living overlapping lives in Akhenaten's reign. One related self is a priestess of Isis. Under Akhenaten's persuasive teachings, she converts to the belief in one God, Ra, the creator of all that is. Akhenaten taught that all other gods and goddesses exist, but are different aspects of Ra, much like we humans are each aspects of our greater souls. For that priestess, that isn't just a belief in her life—it's a reality that she sees and experiences. Perhaps influenced by that related self's profound experiences, I share that belief in this life. (Though I don't use the name Ra; in the mid-1990s, God invited me to call him Joe, and that's how I address him.)

A great serenity arises from that awareness and truth. You can imagine the horror and disgust of the unconverted priests who were left behind during Akhenaten's conversion campaigns. After Akhenaten died, those priests raged back into power and did their best to re-convert all the apostate priests and priestesses who followed Akhenaten, and tried to erase Akhenaten from history.

Some of my related selves' fellow priests and priestesses converted back to the old religion to save their skins, but with Akhenaten's help, my related priestess self had seen a truer reality and couldn't, out of integrity, recant. She was sealed inside a tomb to die. Interestingly, one of her and my related selves living an overlapping life with her is one of the priests who entombed her. After psychokinetically tossing about the tomb furniture in her frustration and anger, she left her body.

I also have related selves living three or four overlapping lives during World War II; one as a nurse in London, one as a Big Band leader-cum-soldier who dies in a plane crash, and one as an infamous Nazi general. (Years ago, I brought through a long message from him as he is now in the afterlife about the Nazis and the death camps, and it was hair raising. It's on my website: https://thelighthouseonline.com/channel/jan23_96.html.) But again, these other lives aren't me; they are related selves, facets of the same greater soul.

## *Reincarnation and animal companions*

I've been present at the death of many beloved kitties. Cats (and dogs and all other animals) are also souls inhabiting bodies, and they leave their bodies a lot more easily than we humans do. Here, I briefly discuss how cats see and experience death, and on how they choose to reincarnate.

Just like us, our animal companions are also each an aspect of a greater soul. That means an animal's soul doesn't return exactly as it was. However, an animal's greater soul can choose to send a similar aspect to share our lives again, returning to the same human in that human's much longer lifespan. And each animal's related self is aware of its other related selves and its greater soul—there isn't the division between our individual selves and our greater souls and related selves that we humans experience. Cats and other animals incarnate the same way we humans do: as an individual expression of the greater soul they belong to. Much like our related selves that are close to other related selves (working on similar life lessons), an animal companion's greater soul can send related souls to be near us.

Aspects of one of my animal companion cats' greater soul have been in my life three times that I know of. For each of her returns, I only became aware after about a year of her being in my life that it was an aspect of the same greater soul. Each time it was a delightful surprise.

The first time she was in my life, I didn't know anything about anything. I just knew I loved her. I'd adopted her from the County of Santa Clara Animal Services Center in the late 1970s. She was a lovely year-old tuxedo with a single orange spot on her shoulder. (A vet later told me she was a "failed calico." He probably thought he was being funny.) The shelter folks told me her human family had surrendered her and her litter mates when they got too old to be cute. The family must have hit her with a broom a lot, because she fled in terror every time I got out my broom to sweep.

I named her Shoshannah, a Hebrew name meaning Lily. Shoshannah was with me for many years until she died a mysterious death in 1988 in Santa Cruz. She was an indoor/outdoor cat and one morning she never came back in. While searching and calling for her, I came across some yard maintenance folks for the condo I was renting. They said they'd found the body of a dead tuxedo cat in the shallow pond outside my rental condo. They'd thrown the body into their garbage. I knew it was Shoshannah. (There's more to this story, but the information isn't relevant to this book and would anyway make me sound absolutely bonkers.)

Fast forward a few years. In 1991, I purchased a pair of purebred Japanese Bobtail kittens the day before the Oakland firestorm erupted. One kitten was a calico I named Keishi (which I thought meant "poppy"; when asking cats psychically what name they want, I've found that girl cats prefer flower names; boy cats prefer fruit and vegetable names. Turns out I got the Japanese spelling of "poppy" wrong). Once, when Keishi was about a year old and came to snuggle with me, I felt her essence and realized she was from the same greater soul that Shoshannah had come from.

Keishi had the same energetic feeling (I call it an energy signature) as Shoshannah had had, though, being an aspect of the same greater soul and not the identical soul, she was also her own cat self. Whether human or animal or plant or souls not in physical bodies, beings each have a unique energy signature that can't be faked. A being can lie and claim to be Lord X of the spiritual realm, but they can't disguise their energy signature, and a sensitive like me can feel the difference, and then they're busted. The converse is true: an incarnated being is its own unique self, and also shares an energy signature with its greater soul. Therefore even though a beloved animal companion looks different and has its own personality, its energy signature from its connection with its greater soul tells me that they are related selves to other cat companions I've had in my life.

Years later, when Keishi was so ill that I made the decision to have her euthanized, she stared at me intently throughout the procedure until she could keep her eyes open no longer. I knew she was trying to tell me something, but I was crying too hard to receive her message.

I've since spoken with beloved animal companions for whom I (or clients) made the brutally hard decision to have euthanized. The interesting answer I've received from those animal companions is that death is different—for cats, at least. They know immediately when we've made the decision to euthanize, and they are eternally forgiving about that decision. They see death as a door through which they choose to come and go. Throughout their lives, they are in connection with their greater souls and with the rest of existence, and don't fear death the same way we disconnected humans do.

In 2009, a few years after Keishi's death, I visited Forgotten Felines of Sonoma County, a cat rescue group that tends feral cat colonies, to adopt a kitten. After looking at all but one of the kittens there, I still hadn't found "the one." The last kitten I picked up was a tiny, scrawny white girl with a black tail and one black ear. She'd been sickly from spay surgery complications, and she looked frail. As soon as I picked her up, she looked up at me adoringly and said clearly (mentally), "At last you've come!"

I adopted her, even though I thought she would only live a few more weeks. Yet against all odds, she thrived. Not knowing who she was, I named her Lily at her request. (Remember that Shoshannah means lily.) It took about a year to realize that Lily was from the same greater soul as Shoshannah and Keishi had been. Lily lived until she was 14. She died at home in October 2023 and her death hit my daughter and me quite hard. Lily told me the day after her death that she would come back again, and asked that we have patience because it would be a while. I assume she meant another aspect from her greater soul would come into our lives.

My fingers are crossed that we will know her when that aspect of her greater soul rejoins us. The cat distribution system will surely come through again.

It's useful to know that our greater souls can choose to send aspects into non-human forms as well, which means that Shoshannah, Keishi, and Lily's greater soul could also be sending aspects into human bodies as well as other forms. From his perspective as a greater soul, Seth (a greater soul channeled by Jane Roberts) once said he had incarnated as a dog in the early 1900s. I think that dog was Strongheart, a German Shepherd who starred in movies in the 1920s. I base this on intuition from having read *Kinship with All Life*, by J. Allen Boone (Harper & Row, 1954).

## *This world is precious and our time in it is brief*

As you may have gathered by now, if you accept this version of reincarnation, we only have this one chance to enjoy physical reality. We can visit it as spirits, but our experiences while in a body are unique and never to be repeated. **Physical reality is precious and to be enjoyed**. Part of enjoying it is knowing that you're being the best person you can be while living here.

We also each have a collection of purposes we are here to accomplish. Some of those purposes might be brief: We are in the right place at the right time to say the right thing to someone who needs to hear what we say. We might not even be consciously aware of that purpose; we just happen to complete the task, or we listen to our intuition and complete the task without knowing why we are doing that thing.

Some of our purposes are longer term, and can either be something we are good at and are intended (by our greater self) to do in this life. Some are life lessons we need to learn, and that might take us our entire lifetime to learn: we might be learning about communication or empathy or how to genuinely care for our fellow human beings. We might be exploring what it means to be a terrible human being, and from the consequences, we learn (sometimes in our life review) to never do anything like that again. Our greater soul assigns us these purposes, though because of free will, we can choose to do other things as well, or we can refuse to work on our purposes.

I was asked by someone who read this book in manuscript form to explain why some babies die so soon after birth. What is their purpose? Is an exception made for those souls? Do they get another chance at living a human life in physical reality? Since I've never been asked to communicate with such a soul, I asked the question psychically of my spiritual contacts. The answer I received is that the souls inhabiting those babies were sent by their greater selves to help others and to briefly experience some aspects of human life. After bodily death, they return to their greater soul to report on their experiences, from which the greater soul and all related selves learn. Although it seems unfair, they are not sent back to earth to live a longer life; their greater soul's reasons for incarnating as that baby, however briefly, have been accomplished.

# Chapter 9
# Thinking about suicide as an escape?

As I say at the very beginning of this book, there is nothing to fear from death. There is also no reason to rush toward it. We are each unique. We are each precious. We are each irreplaceable. And quite importantly, we are each needed. As I explain in chapter 8, we have never been on this earth before, nor will we ever be here again. Other aspects of our greater self are on this earth in various times and places, but none of those other selves, nor us, will ever live another physical life.

*Figure 26. Doing away with ourselves is as destructive as an atomic blast.*

If you are thinking you would be better off dead, especially after reading that everyone goes to heaven and nobody is judged or condemned to a non-existent hell, please, please think again, and seek help. Although everything may seem hopeless, there are countless humans ready to help. That help may not be perfect, but then no human is ever perfect. Take advantage of that help. I list some resources at the end of this chapter.

## *Suicide is not a reset button*

Some people feel that they've failed this life, or that they're nothing but trouble for others, or that life is horrible and painful and has no purpose, and that they would do everyone and themselves a favor by taking themselves out of the equation by killing themselves. If they believe in classical reincarnation, they think they then get to redo it all. That's not the case.

Suicide is irrevocable. It's a terrible mistake. It's not a do-over or a rest button, it's an "abandon mission." Even if classical reincarnation is true and you as you are now get to be reborn in another life, the situations, people, and environments you'd be in would be different. Despite what William Shakespeare wrote, life is not a literal play where we all have assigned roles, actions, and dialog. Instead, with free will, we are self-directing and can say and do as we wish. The Roman Catholic church once classified suicide as a mortal sin—that is, as a mistake that separates us from the Divine. (The church removed suicide from being a mortal sin in 1983.) I like to think they classified it as a mortal sin because they understood what a mistake it is, and were doing what they could to prevent people from doing themselves in.

I've spoken with several people in the afterlife who committed suicide. Without exception, each has regretted their actions and realizes they made a terrible mistake.

Why?

Because, as I explain in chapter 8, you as you are on this earth right now have never been here before, and you will never be here again. If you remove yourself from physical life, you deprive yourself of many opportunities, opportunities that you'll never have again in the same way, and you deprive others of the things they could have experienced and learned when interacting with you were you still alive.

Let's examine what happens when someone commits suicide, and the harm that suicide does to the world and to the person killing themselves.

When a person commits suicide, they take themselves out of the complex web of existence of which they are a part. All the people they know, all the people they would have come to know, all the encounters they would have had, move out of the realm of the actual. What could have been is no longer possible. The people you might have been able to help with a simple smile or a few kind words no longer have you there to help. The people you might have helped in the longer term simply by being you also no longer have you there to help. Any purpose you came to earth to accomplish remains forever undone.

I won't go into multiverses and alternate realities—the details get too complex and don't affect what you do in the here and now. Yes, an alternate version of you most likely exists in another dimension, but it isn't the same soul as you and is instead another aspect of your greater soul.

**I cannot overemphasize how special and important you are, exactly as you are now.**

Think of your existence as a presence woven into a complex, living tapestry. The threads from which you are woven are connected to everything else in that tapestry. Killing yourself is like cutting out that area of the tapestry you are in. It severs all those complex connections you have with everyone and everything else in the tapestry—not just humans, but other forms of life as well. The people and other lifeforms whose presence you supported simply by existing no longer have that support; the people to whom you might have given opportunities to learn and grow no longer have you to give those opportunities.

*Figure 27. Suicide tears a you-shaped hole in the tapestry of physical reality. The tapestry repairs itself, but it isn't and can't be the same.*

## *Help is here, but we don't always recognize it*

Yet this tale of the tapestry is just an analogy. Life isn't a flat, inanimate tapestry; it's alive and ever changing. When you tear yourself out of the tapestry of life, life weaves in new threads, new people, to connect with those people you tore yourself away from, so those people get experiences similar to what they would have gotten from you. Those experiences aren't the same —they never could be, as you are unique—but they provide the same kinds of things those other people need. Those experiences are always an opportunity for those people to learn and grow. Those folks might not take advantage of the opportunity, but at least life brings to us what we need.

What do I mean by opportunity? Let's say a person is self-centered and only thinks of themselves; maybe even feels entitled to take what they want from others without regard for balance or a fair exchange. Another person might come into their lives who doesn't let themselves be used. This gives the taker the opportunity to reflect on their attitudes and behavior and make themselves a better person. The taker might not see the experience as an opportunity, and in fact is most likely to complain, play the victim, and blame the person who won't allow themselves to be used instead of realizing they themselves need to change, but they can't later say they weren't given a chance. ("Later" might only come when they do their life review in the afterlife.) Some people ignore the help and opportunities sent to them, or refuse to recognize that they have help or an opportunity because what comes to them doesn't look like what they expected, then complain that they never received any help.

Complaining that one never received help is like the joke about the person caught in a flood.

Before a flood, news stations on television, radio, phone apps, and the internet warn everyone in the area of the possibility of the flood, and advise everyone to evacuate from low-lying areas. Most people do, but one person, whose house is near a river, stays home, saying, "I have faith that the Lord will provide."

Later, their neighbors come by and say, "We're evacuating and have room in our car. Come along with us!"

The person refuses, saying they don't need to. "The Lord will provide."

Then the sheriff comes knocking on the door. "The river is rising and your house will soon be flooded. Get out! Evacuate now!"

Again, the person says, "I don't need to. The Lord will provide."

The waters rise, forcing the person to retreat to the roof. A person in a rowboat comes by and says, "Hop in!"

Again, the person says, "The Lord will provide." The person in the rowboat leaves.

Finally, a helicopter hovers above the roof and dangles a rope. "This is your last chance! Climb up!"

Yet again the person refuses, saying, "The Lord will provide."

The waters continue to rise and the inevitable happens. The person dies and goes to the afterlife. When he arrives, he seeks out the Lord and berates him, saying, "What kind of God are you? I believed in you! I trusted that you would provide! Yet you did nothing!"

To which the Lord replies, "I sent you news warnings, neighbors, a sheriff, a rowboat, and a helicopter. You refused all my help. What more could I have done?"

The point of this joke is that we often don't recognize help when it comes to us, because it isn't in the form we expect. Have an open mind and be willing to try to see how someone, some opportunity, or some situation is help, even if it's not what we expect. Learn to say "yes" to life more often and see where it takes you. But don't say "yes" blindly. Use discernment and common sense.

## *We are here on earth for many reasons*

We are all on this earth for many reasons. We often don't know why. Or we think we know why, but are frequently wrong because we assign outward, physical reality reasons. ("I'm here to make money," or "I'm here to be successful," or "I'm here to be popular.") Those could be a few of the reasons for us being here, but seldom are the most meaningful reasons.

More usually, some of our multiple purposes for being may be as simple as being a kind, compassionate voice when someone most needs it. Or to be in the right place with the right knowledge at the right time so we can say one sentence to a person that is exactly what they needed to hear.

Here's an example. A neighbor's husband died unexpectedly, and their daughter took out her grief on her mother by blaming her and accusing her of having been a bad wife.

When my neighbor told me this, without knowing the particulars, I listened to an inner nudge and said to her, "Every relationship has conflict. That doesn't mean it's a bad relationship. What matters is how you manage that conflict. If you manage the conflict lovingly and with respect, it's a good relationship."

My neighbor's eyes lit up and she said, "Exactly!" A certain tension eased out of her body, and I realized that I had said what she needed to hear. If I hadn't listened to my intuition (it could have been her husband from the afterlife prompting me), she would have gotten the information another way, but perhaps not as clearly or as soon.

As we learn to listen to our intuition and inner guidance, we help each other through these kinds of interactions every day. Even if we don't consciously know we're "supposed" to say something, if we spontaneously say something that's on our mind (as long as it's true and kind—and sometimes being kind means saying an unpleasant truth), we help those around us.

As an aside, if you decide to listen to your intuition, it isn't as easy as saying to yourself, "I have a feeling I should do X, so I'll do it." Unless person is reasonably self-aware and rational, they can often conflate their hopes, fears, and opinions with their genuine intuitively received information. I once knew someone who had a psychic gift, but she ran more on her emotions than on rationality, and was not in any way self-reflecting or self-aware. So she would warn people against something when in fact it was just her attempt to control those people, or she would say something good was going to happen when in fact she was in denial about the facts and she was just conveying her hopes. Occasionally she would be correct, which lead those around her to take all her warnings and predictions more seriously.

When we speak up to someone, what we say might not have an immediate effect. Instead, we might be planting seeds for that person to think on later, when they are ready. On occasion, "when they are ready" means in their afterlife. I give one example of messages only getting recognized in the afterlife in chapter 14. Sometimes we need to draw boundaries and tell people that what they are doing is harming us and is therefore not okay. Sometimes we need to say something, then walk away to protect ourselves from further harm. Other times we are messengers, bringing information to someone for their use. It's not up to us to "make" anyone think anything or do anything or respond to what we say, nor is it up to us to decide what's best for someone else or to step on their agency in making their own decisions.

Here's an example of speaking up. One time while eating at a local fish and chips shop, I overheard a young woman complaining to her friends about an abusive relationship she was in. She said that because she didn't love herself, she was incapable of loving anyone else. This is a hugely abusive lie. A person who doesn't love themselves is fully capable of loving others. It's just that they unconsciously choose to love abusive people because they think that's all they deserve.

When she was standing in line to pay, I approached her and said I'd overheard what she said. I told her she was fully capable of loving people, and had only been loving abusive people because that was all she believed she deserved, and that she deserved better. She looked startled and a bit upset, so I said nothing more and walked away. It could be she thought I was blaming her for her choices (I wasn't), or it could be she just wasn't ready to let go of blaming herself. But I want to think that eventually she realized that she was, in fact, capable of loving others and deserved to be treated better. In the moment, I said what I was prompted to say and let go of the outcome.

This was one of the first lessons I learned when I started doing psychic readings for others—letting go of the outcome. At times when I brought through information that I knew was correct and helpful (correct information has a certain energetic feel to it), a client would agree with what I said and say they knew they should act on the information. But then they wouldn't act on it, or they would argue with me and tell me reasons why they couldn't do it (this is called the "Yes, but" game, in which a person takes delight in complaining about a situation, then shooting down all suggestions; Eric Berne describes this game in his book *Games People Play*, cited in chapter 6), or they would do the opposite of what I advised them was the best course.

At first this frustrated me. It was reminiscent of the quote, "To know, and not to do, is to not know." That is, if you say you know something requires action, yet you don't act on that knowledge, you don't truly know or understand that "something." (The quote is variously attributed to Lao Tzu; Johann Wolfgang von Goethe; and Leo Buscaglia, from whom I first heard the phrase. I haven't been able to find a credible source. Nonetheless, the quote itself is valid.)

I didn't like feeling stressed and frustrated after these kinds of readings, so I decided to do something about it by doing some inner work. It was hard, but I taught myself to let go of worrying about whether my clients would do anything with the information I passed along to them. That decision required compassion for myself and my clients. Letting go of caring about the outcome is good practice for life in general.

The takeaway here is that you may never know when you've been useful and have helped others, but you can be assured that by your very existence, you have a reason for being here and a purpose to fulfill. So please don't take yourself away; too many people need you.

## *If you need to make an end-of-life decision*

An end-of-life decision is one you make when you have a terminal illness and want to die with dignity. In those cases, you can seek medical help. Some states in the US have "death with dignity" laws that allow people with terminal illnesses to legally commit suicide with physician assistance.

Physician-assisted suicide is a separate issue from self-inflicted suicide. Although suicide has been decriminalized in many countries, committing suicide is still illegal in some countries. That includes physician-assisted suicide, which is only legal in a handful of places. Of course, it's impossible to prosecute a person who has successfully killed themselves, but their family suffers not just emotionally, but legally as well. And if a person isn't successful at killing themselves, they are in legal trouble, and possibly experience lasting health problems from the failed suicide attempt, further adding to the misery that caused them to seek an end to their lives in the first place.

Although I know full well how it feels to despair of life so deeply that you wish to kill yourself, I cannot imagine the anguish required to make an end-of-life decision for quality of life reasons. I have never spoken with someone in the afterlife who made this decision, so I cannot speak about what it's like. I have no advice to offer in this situation beyond this: Whatever decision you make about physician-assisted suicide is yours to make, but please consider it fully.

## *Resources and help for those considering suicide*

If you or someone you know is thinking of suicide, reach out to someone you trust and care for. But be careful, and use good judgment. If you're feeling suicidal, it could be the very people you trust who are making your life miserable. Sometimes we trust those whom we should never trust. Childhood trauma can set us up in such a way that we allow abusive people in our lives because we don't believe we deserve any better.

If you have no trustworthy person in your life, reach out to any of the following resources. This list isn't exhaustive. If your country isn't on the list or isn't on the international hot line website, many countries use 911, 999, or 112. If that doesn't work, use Google to find resources in your country. If you don't have access to the internet, local libraries often provide computers you can use. If you call a hotline and aren't happy with the results, call again. Help is there for you. Take the time to find it. Persevere until you get the help you want. Your life is worth it, and suicide is irrevocable.

- Canada: 911
- Canada Kids Help Line: 1-800-668-6868
- UK: 116 123
- USA: 911
- USA Suicide & Crisis Lifeline (formerly known as the National Suicide Prevention Lifeline): 988
- USA Crisis Text Line: 1-800-273-8255 (TALK), or text HOME to 741741
- USA suicide and crisis websites: https://988lifeline.org, https://crisistextline.org, https://samaritans.org, and https://suicidepreventionlifeline.org
- International list of suicide hot lines around the world: https://blog.opencounseling.com/suicide-hotlines/

# Chapter 10
# Ancestors and the afterlife

It may surprise you that I'm writing about ancestors in a book about life after death. It surprised me—I hadn't originally planned to say anything about ancestors—but in the context of what I know and have experienced as a psychic and a medium over many decades, it makes complete sense.

Genealogists use the term "ancestor" to mean everyone from whom you are biologically descended—your parents, your grandparents, and so on. Your brothers and sisters and aunts and uncles and cousins and great aunts and great uncles and so on aren't ancestors, though they *are* family. (Ancestors include the non-parental events—NPEs, meaning people whose fathers or mothers aren't the ones officially recorded as their parents. That happens far more often than you may suspect, and if you have an NPE in your family tree, the people who were the actual parent in your direct line are your ancestors as well.)

When speaking of ancestors, there's no such thing as not having any family. Regardless of whether you can trace your ancestry back any distance, your ancestors exist. Somebody fathered you and somebody gave birth to you, so you have parents. Your parents have parents. Your parents' parents have parents. And so on.

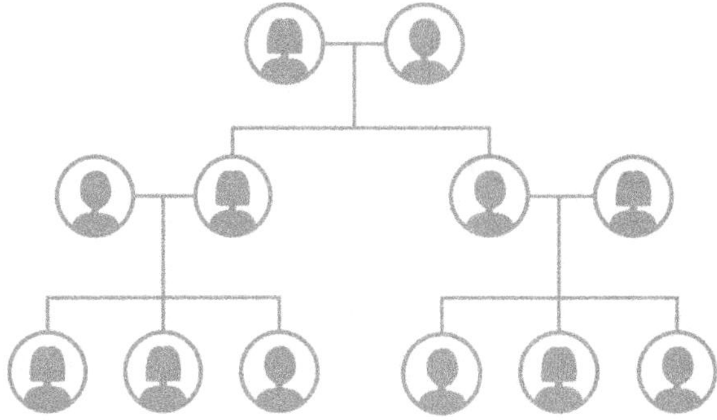

*Figure 28. A family tree. Everyone has ancestors.*

Looking at ancestors from a cultural perspective, for many cultures, ancestors include those from whom everyone in your cultural group is descended. That includes both your biological ancestors as well as people who lived in the same cultural group as your family in previous generations. I consider those to be ancestors as well.

As discussed elsewhere in this book, people who have left their physical bodies are still alive in the afterlife (most of them; some have moved on to other adventures—life after the afterlife, if you will). That statement includes those of your ancestors who remain in the afterlife. Therefore it makes sense to talk about your ancestors in a book on the afterlife.

I say "remain in the afterlife" because once a soul moves on from the afterlife, they've evolved so much, including multidimensionally, that they are interested in larger concerns and are no longer so deeply invested in helping their descendants. Although some of them may still be accessible to communication, the types of topics they'll want to discuss with you are going to be very high level indeed, and you'll need to have become a reasonably evolved human being to be interested in (and able to understand) what they have to say. They're for sure not going to want to discuss whether your Aunt Mary's potato salad was better than your Uncle Matt's potato salad. (In case the humor is lost, some highly evolved beings in fact will indulge you in discussions of potato salad wars, but they're going to couch their messages in terms of love and certainly aren't going to take sides. If you perceive them as taking sides, that's your projection arising out of your level of evolution, not a true representation of their thoughts.)

## *Why consult with your ancestors?*

However you define what an ancestor is, why might you want to consult with your ancestors? You'll need to know a bit more about your ancestors' existence to understand the answer.

Because of our multidimensional existence, people who have left their physical bodies are still alive in their times. That includes our ancestors. What do I mean when I say they are still alive in their times? I mean that ancestor that lived on earth is (a) still alive on earth as a soul in a human body in their time and place and also, simultaneously, (b) alive in the afterlife or wherever they chose to go after the afterlife.

You can connect with your ancestors both in the afterlife and on earth. When connecting with them on earth, you connect with them in the time in which they are still alive on earth, and those connections can be useful. In my experience as a psychic, I've often helped people by talking with their ancestors or with related selves as those ancestors or related selves are in their places and times. The process is simple and usually has only taken one session to clear up whatever was resonating in this lifetime from those other people's lifetimes. Communication with an ancestor can also bring enlightening information about a family dynamic.

However, for simplicity's sake, in this chapter, I stay focused on your ancestors as they are alive in the afterlife, not as they are alive on earth in their time, and explain from that perspective why it's helpful to connect with your ancestors in the afterlife.

## *How can ancestors help?*

Many people and cultures speak of honoring your ancestors and reaching out to them for wisdom and advice. I had heard and read about this practice, yet even though I assumed there was truth to those beliefs, I was uninterested in my ancestors because all my grandparents were terrible human beings. It was like a firewall of abuse preventing me from looking further. My reasoning was this: Why would I want to connect with abusive people in the afterlife? They weren't good people in life, and they sure aren't going to have suddenly evolved into decent beings in the afterlife—that takes dedicated effort of the kind I doubted any of those ancestors were interested in.

In short, I wrote off my entire extensive set of ancestors just because my immediate ancestors were terrible people.

In 2021, my interest in ancestors was piqued by Nancy Hendrickson's book, *Ancestral Tarot* (Weiser Books, 2021). In that book, Hendrickson offers a wealth of exercises you can do with tarot cards to find out more about your ancestors, and to contact the ones you want to talk with. If you're a Christian and the mention of tarot cards frightens you, be aware that tarot arose out of Christian cultures in 14th century Europe and is still rife with Christian symbols and imagery. It's only recently that some religions have decided to condemn tarot as an evil implement of the devil. After all, tarot is a tool you can use to communicate more clearly with the Divine. People who want to control you don't want you to connect directly to the Divine and get Divine guidance; you might discover that you've been told some porky pies (lies) by those people who want to control you. In those people's minds, it's better to convince you that a tool is evil and to gaslight you into not trusting any information you receive through that tool. Though it is also true that the creator of a tarot deck imbues their energies into the deck, and sometimes those energies are dark and ill-intentioned. So use your intuition, discernment, and judgment when choosing a tarot deck.

In Hendrickson's book, she acknowledges that yes, some ancestors are terrible, but most of our ancestors were not, and those who are not terrible are ready, willing, and able to help us better understand ourselves.

Using Hendrickson's book to connect with my ancestors, I was joyfully surprised to find that hey, most of my ancestors aren't like my grandparents; instead, they are better beings who are interested (some are keenly interested) in helping me continue to heal from the abuse I'd suffered. This was a revelation and a relief, and in retrospect, I realized that I had rejected hundreds of thousands of ancestors because of the evil deeds of just a few. I'm sure many of your ancestors will likewise celebrate the healing you've done, and will want to help you continue to heal.

You don't have to connect with your ancestors. But if you find yourself drawn to the idea of connecting with your ancestors, even if you don't need help from them, you can still connect with them for other reasons. Here are some of those reasons.

There's a theory that certain memories are passed down genetically—that some experiences affect not just the person experiencing them, but their descendants as well. For example, researchers have found that fear of certain smells is passed down through several mouse generations (Linda Geddes, "Fear of a smell can be passed down several generations," https://www.newscientist.com/article/dn24677-fear-of-a-smell-can-be-passed-down-several-generations/, retrieved October 26, 2024). If you're drawn to this theory that some fears can be passed down through generations, you can perhaps find out more from your ancestors. It could shed some light on things about yourself that have puzzled you.

Another reason is that just as with anyone who has left the earthly plane, ancestors aren't suddenly all wise and all knowing. But they do know your family history, so they can offer insight into family or personal traits that have puzzled you. And the ancestors who have done their homework in the afterlife can offer some guidance for moving out of family trauma, especially generational trauma or other unhealthy family dynamics.

By "homework," I mean ancestors who have been doing their inner work in the afterlife, working on becoming better beings in the same ways I discuss elsewhere in this book.

Think of those homework-doing ancestors as wise ones you can learn from. They won't usually need your help, but they can help you. Their help can come in the form of information and support. Your wise ancestors can even help the less wise ancestors, the ones who are themselves traumatized or who traumatized you, and who haven't learned to be better beings. I recommend against trying to connect with the less wise ones yourself, but just as you can do for any being or situation, you can ask on their behalf that they receive the help they need.

## *Why avoid abusive ancestors?*

Why do I recommend that you avoid the traumatized and recalcitrant ancestors? When connecting with my ancestors, I found to my surprise that even some who have been in the spirit realm a long time are still stubbornly refusing to grow or change. I talked earlier about my paternal grandfather and his father, both of whom were abusive when walking the earth and who are still in the special school I've talked about. They're refusing to even do their life reviews. Even if it were possible to talk with them, they would have nothing useful or helpful to say, and might even try to further their abuse (though they won't be allowed to).

As Beverly Engle says in her book, *The Emotionally Abused Woman* (Ballantine Books, 1992), people abuse others for two reasons: Either they were abused and can't stop themselves from abusing others, or they enjoy abusing others and don't want to stop. In either case, they can't and won't stop abusing others. She says the former might benefit from years and years of therapy so that eventually, they become slightly better toward others, but the latter will never change. Not only can you not help such people, it's detrimental to everyone involved, and unethical, to allow them to continue to abuse you.

On earth, you can walk away from the abusers (though that can be difficult). When dealing with those in the afterlife, you can choose to not engage with them. (And often, they won't be allowed to engage with you even if you wanted to; instead, you can obtain information about them from other sources if that information would be helpful.) This advice applies to ancestors as well. Unless the abusive ones have done an enormous amount of inner work in the afterlife's special school and have finally evolved out of their desire to be abusive, abusive ancestors are still abusers. I'm not saying they won't have changed. But unless you know for sure they've done that work, there's no reason to connect with them.

If a person was abusive when on earth and hasn't changed their tune in the afterlife, they're going to try to be abusive to you and anyone else who tries to connect with them. That is, if they are even allowed to talk with you, which, because of free will, they can if you insist. I recommend you don't insist. While still in an abusive state of being, there is nothing they can say that will be helpful to you.

If you feel you must connect with a specific abusive ancestor, instead of doing it directly, use a safe, skilled intermediary, such as a compassionate, ethical psychic.

### *Many ancestors are evolved and want to help*

Although some ancestors are best avoided, the wise ones among our ancestors can be tremendously helpful and can help you better understand yourself and your place in your family. And although it isn't your job to help your ancestors heal, you can ask your wiser ancestors for help in assisting those in your ancestry who haven't done their homework.

The wise ancestors might not be able to help recalcitrant ancestors to start moving forward, but even then, whatever help the wise ones can offer will be useful at a meta level—the level that tells the recalcitrant ancestors that someone cares. Those recalcitrant ancestors know already that someone cares because their guardian angels have been reassuring them of this since forever, but some souls need to hear that message repeatedly and from many sources for them to finally decide to accept it. And some benighted souls have been so lost in their private misery that they haven't been able to see the help and love around them.

So asking your wise ancestors to help the less wise ones is useful. And asking your wise ancestors to help you is likewise useful. It's one of the many avenues of help available to you. Which avenues you take are up to your preferences and inclinations.

## *Resources for connecting with your ancestors*

Many books have been written on connecting with and working with your ancestors. I'm not an expert, so I've only written at a high level about your ancestors and why you might want to connect with some (and why I recommend that you steer clear of others). If you want to pursue this line of inquiry, I recommend these resources.

1. Daniel Foor, *Ancestral Medicine: Rituals for Personal and Family Healing* (Bear & Company, 2017).
2. If you enjoy using tarot cards as a way to more easily access archetypal information, I recommend these two books by Nancy Hendrickson: *Ancestral Tarot* (Weiser Books, 2021) and *Ancestral Grimoire* (Weiser Books, 2022).

# Chapter 11
# Talking with people about the afterlife

I've sometimes witnessed people who stayed in their bodies after their body died. One time, years ago, I attended the open-casket funeral of an acquaintance's mother. I had a front-row seat and watched, a bit horrified, as the mother tried repeatedly to make her body work. She kept sitting up in the casket, but her body wouldn't follow. She would lie back down, then rise again, trying again and again to make her body work. She'd remained in her body after bodily death because she was terrified of what was going to happen to her in the afterlife.

I spoke to her psychically, giving a modification of the talk I give souls who are possessing other people. (I describe the talk in detail in chapter 13.) I explained to her that her body was dead, but that she wasn't. That she was an immortal soul. That she didn't have to stay on the physical plane, and that she had nothing to fear from the afterlife. That she had a wonderful place to go. After that, she left, to my relief and I'm sure hers.

That wasn't the only time I knew of a soul who stayed stuck in their bodies. It's reassuring to know that someone will always come to help, though some souls choose to ignore the helpers that come for them. In those cases, they either hang around the place where their bodies are interred, or they try to possess a living being. I talk about these kinds of events and that kind of possession in chapter 13.

## *Preparing to talk with someone about their beliefs*

If you know someone who is going to die, one of the kindest and most loving things you can do for them—and the simplest—is to speak with them about their beliefs about the afterlife. I strongly emphasize that you shouldn't do this without researching how to do it. The ideas and suggestions in this chapter are merely a starting point. You can find plenty of resources online or in books for this practice. For example, you could read Elisabeth Kübler-Ross's book, *On Death and Dying: What the Dying Have to Teach Doctors, Nurses, Clergy and Their Own Families*

(Scribner reissue edition, 2014). Dr. Kübler-Ross introduced the concept of the five stages of death: denial and isolation, anger, bargaining, depression, and acceptance. (These stages can also apply when facing other unwanted experiences. In both cases, death or other situations, the stages aren't linear, can overlap, and can repeat. For example, a person might experience both anger and depression, and might come to acceptance, but later return to anger.)

If that book is a bit heavy going, which it can be, search online for the term "palliative care." Or ask your local librarian to help you find such resources on death and dying.

If it's an emergency and someone is dying, you don't have time to find out how to do it in the way prescribed by the experts. In such cases, use your judgment and listen to what your heart tells you to do.

If the person you want to speak with has dementia, that could be an even more important reason to talk with them about death. Even if they don't seem to hear you or understand what you're saying, their soul both hears and understands. Jane Roberts once brought through a message from the entity Seth about dementia. He said that people who experience dementia are so bone-deep frightened of death that they gradually withdraw their attention from the world. That way they aren't aware of (or are less aware of) their impending death. If you speak with them (or perhaps read reassuring things to them, such as this book), they might not be aware, but their soul is, and that can help ease their transition into the next stage of living.

When speaking about death with someone who is more cognizant of their surroundings and is dying, either immediately or soon (because of a terminal illness), be gentle. Ask them questions. What do they believe is going to happen after bodily death? Why do they believe that? Are they open to a different perspective? Don't lecture them, don't try to frighten them with threats of eternal damnation. Listen to what they say. If they think there's nothing after death, ask more questions, and if it seems appropriate, state what you believe as non-denominationally as you can. Avoid giving advice. If someone is terminally ill, avoid saying that "you're going to recover," or "everything is going to be all right." (Unless you make it clear that you're talking about the outcome for their soul after bodily death.) Talking honestly about a person's hopes and fears is far more helpful.

I recommend this approach because even if it seems you aren't making an impression, the person you're speaking with will recognize, at least subconsciously, any truth in what you say, and they will remember the discussion when their body dies, so they are much less likely to stay stuck in their body after bodily death, and more likely to see the help that is there to get them to the next step in their lives.

## *Begin with questions about some core beliefs*

When starting to talk with someone about the afterlife, the goal is not to push your beliefs onto that person. The goal is to listen to them and to help them think through their beliefs. Everyone has beliefs; often those beliefs are unconscious and they've never thought about them. Asking questions can help them become more aware of their unconscious beliefs. Let them lead the conversation. Let the conversation roam. As I've shown in this book, talking about the afterlife can mean talking about all aspects of life.

It can be helpful to start with easier, less challenging topics. In a few paragraphs, I give some sample questions you can ask someone about their core beliefs. Sometimes these questions will be entirely new to them; they may have been dreaming their way through life without thinking about any of these things. Though (and maybe I'm being idealistic), it's unlikely that the person you're talking with hasn't considered at least some of these questions, so they should already have answers and will, one hopes, be comfortable with, and possibly even enjoy, discussing these questions.

It can be interesting to ask yourself these questions, too, or, when discussing the questions with others, to have a round-robin discussion in which each person shares their thoughts and ideas. There are no wrong answers or beliefs.

Perhaps you can mention what Joseph Campbell said in his book, *The Power of Myth*: "One of the psychological problems in growing old is the fear of death. ... But this body is a vehicle of consciousness, and if you can identify with the consciousness, you can watch this body go like an old car. There goes the fender, there goes the tire, one thing after another –but it's predictable. And then, gradually, the whole thing drops off, and consciousness rejoins consciousness. It is no longer in this particular environment."

*Figure 29. Joseph Campbell makes an analogy of our bodies as we age as a car that is falling apart. The car represents our bodies. When the car is inoperable, we, the soul driving the car, continue.*

When asking these questions, don't rush through them. You may find even one question sparks a lively, lengthy discussion. Take the time needed to talk about these questions and the attendant answers. In one sense, there are no right or wrong answers; just discovering one's own answers is going to be enormously helpful.

- What is important to you in human interactions?
- What do you value? Do you value kindness? Fairness? Openness? Honesty? Command? Control? Power? Domination over others? Always being right?
- What does "respect" mean to you? Do you treat yourself and others with respect?
- Are material objects important to you? How important? More important than people and personal values? Less important? Are there some people who are not worth as much as some material objects or money?
- What does it mean to you to say that someone has character?
- What about integrity—what does that mean to you?
- Do you have a lot of core values and rules you live by, or just a few, or somewhere in between? What are they?
- What do you do when someone challenges your core values either by word or deed?
- What do you do when you are tempted to act against your core values? How do you feel when you resist temptation and

do what you feel is right? Or when you don't resist temptation and do something you feel is wrong?

The next set of questions dives more deeply into beliefs about our existence. As you ask these questions and discuss the answers, you may find the person's ideas changing during the discussion or over the course of a few discussions. That's good, because it shows that the person you're talking with is flexible and adaptable enough to accept new ideas. That bodes well for them in the afterlife.

- What do you believe about dreams? Are they biochemical reactions, a result of something you ate? Or are dreams sometimes something more than a biochemical reaction?
- Can you connect with others in your dreams? Can you receive messages in your dreams? Many people believe they receive dream messages from loved ones who have died from this earth. Do you believe that's possible? Why or why not?
- What do you believe you are? Are you a body and nothing more? Are you a soul inhabiting and operating a body? Do you believe you have a soul that's separate from your conscious mind? What is the soul?
- Do you believe that our senses aren't to be trusted? If so, why?
- Do you believe in an afterlife? If so, what do you believe? Are your beliefs based in a religion, or did you develop them yourself?
- Do you believe in heaven and hell, or something like those places? If so, what do you believe about those places? What are they like? How do you get there? Where do your beliefs about those places come from? Are they from family or your cultural heritage, or did you adopt them on your own?

If someone seems determined to believe that something bad is going to happen to them after bodily death, ask them why they believe that. (For that matter, it's a good practice to ask yourself why you're willing to believe something.)

One essential but scary question to only ask if it seems appropriate: "Are you afraid of dying? Why or why not?" Some people are terrified of death, and asking this question might not help alleviate their fears. The earlier questions I've given are much gentler and can get us thinking in a sideways fashion about the core topic, which is our bodily death.

More questions to ask include

- What is free will, and what does it have to do with anything?
- What do you believe about free will? Do you believe we have the freedom to choose? Do you think that someone or something divine makes choices for you? Do you believe, as the American psychologist B. F. Skinner did, that there is no such thing as free will, and that instead all we think and feel arises from our physical existence, and that our actions are nothing more than the result of previous actions?

For more ideas you can discus, see chapter 4 (on free will), chapter 6 (on emotions), and chapter 8 (on reincarnation).

# Chapter 12
# What matters and what doesn't matter

Before you read the rest of this chapter, I ask that you bear in mind this truth about yourself (and all of us): We are perfect right now, as who and what we are. Unless we are in deep, deep denial about ourselves (and some people are), we're aware of our flaws and we often feel less than acceptable for having them. But those flaws are a necessary part of ourselves. Therefore we shouldn't reject ourselves because of those flaws, but should instead see them as opportunities to become better human beings while at the same time appreciating ourselves as we are. We're like kittens. Kittens (or puppies, if you prefer) are perfect as they are, despite still needing to mature and learn to control their claws and teeth. They continue to be perfect as they grow and mature.

As possibly said by Portuguese poet Fernando Pessoa (1888-1935) in "Palco de vida" ("Stages of Life"), "You can have flaws, be anxious and even be angry, but don't forget that your life is the greatest business in the world. Only you can stop it from failure. You are appreciated, admired, and loved by many. Remember that being happy is not a sky without storms, a road without accidents, a job without effort, relationships without disappointment." (This attribution has not been verified, and the text is often falsely put in the late Pope Francis's mouth. Also, the passage is much longer than I've quoted. I recommend you look it up so you can read the entire passage.)

If you look at us as immortal souls enjoying a temporary physical existence, after which we move on to a permanent non-physical existence, then all the following is true.

- When our bodies die, we only take with us two things: what we've made of ourselves as human beings, and the relationships we've created with other people.
- Material things don't matter.
- Outward appearance doesn't matter.
- Wealth, power, influence—none of them matter. They can be enjoyable, but they don't matter.

What does matter is the kind of person you are and how you treat your fellow human beings (and the rest of earth as well).

In that light, it makes sense that doing the required inner work to become a better human being should be a high priority now—at least in your list of your top ten priorities. In case you haven't heard the term, or in case you have a different definition, "inner work" means examining yourself, your actions, and your motivations and doing what you can to correct your faults so you become a better human being. To do inner work, you need to be self-aware and responsible. Being self-aware means being aware of what you're doing, why you're doing it, and how what you're doing affects others. Being responsible means accepting that you are in charge of yourself and that you aren't the victim of circumstances.

Yet doing inner work means facing a lot of truths about yourself, some of which are uncomfortable and cringey. For some of us, there aren't that many cringe-inducing truths; for others, there are so many that we fear that all we are is unworthy; that we're terrible human beings with no redeeming qualities, and we might as well give up and keep on truckin' on, rejecting inner inspection, continuing to do what we've always done, and not trying to better ourselves in any meaningful way. When carried to an extreme, this rejection of our responsibility to improve ourselves can lead to us diving deeper into denial and creating false memories to cover up what has really happened.

There are any number of reasons for creating false memories. The most common reason is a combination of fear, denial, and projection. People create false memories when they feel deeply uncomfortable with how they behaved and they don't want to be accountable, so they create a new narrative in which they never did any of those bad things and are instead the hero. These false memories can be a part of what's called narcissistic amnesia, but non-narcissists also go into denial, "forget" the truth, and create false memories as well.

False memories are often provably false, but the person with false memories has a vested interest in resisting the facts that could correct their memories. They resist because, if they give up the false memory and accept what really happened, they must face their regret and start working on becoming a better human being, which might include apologizing and making amends. Even when given proof that their memories are false, they might temporarily admit the truth, but often return to telling themselves and others the lie they prefer. They just don't feel strong enough to accept responsibility for their actions, and so they are afraid of doing any inner work.

And as Carl Jung discovered to his bemusement, many people just don't want to work that hard; they're afraid of what they'll find out about themselves and that they aren't capable of being better people. And it can be a lot, to let the scales fall from our eyes and to look on what we've done. We usually don't know that looking at ourselves, even the uncomfortable parts, doesn't mean we aren't capable of being better people; in fact, it's the only way to become better.

Not knowing that, we instead focus on the material world, which offers a much easier outward measure of our worth: wealth, status, power, looks, influence.

But seeking material things to prove our worth is pointless. We are all worthy in the eyes of our creators. In the world of the divine, none of us is judged or will be judged except by ourselves; no one is condemned, though the worst of us must undergo some post-death education in how to be responsible. Nobody is punished. There is no hell. There is no eternal damnation; that's an invention by human beings possibly arising out of the desire to believe that bad people will be punished, and most certainly arising out of the desire to control others through fear of the divine.

You may ask, reasonably, why bother to try to be a better human being? If there is no punishment, no hell, no eternal damnation, why not coast as you are until death, then take what comes after? Why not put off what you aren't required to do? Why bother now if the worst you'll face in the afterlife is some indeterminate amount of time in some kind of school for souls in which the lessons, though mandatory, can be done at your own pace?

I don't know how to answer what are to me nonsensical questions. I don't know how to convince someone who doesn't want to be a better human being how to want to be one, or why they should want to. I can give you the information, but I can't think for you and I can't draw conclusions for you. I can only leave it to you to answer the questions for yourself.

For the most succinct opinion, I remind you of what Desmond Tutu and his daughter Mpho Tutu said in their book, *Made for Goodness* (HarperOne, 2010): "opting for the easy wrong may save the body, but it kills the soul."

Or as Dante says in line 115 of Canto XXVIII of *The Inferno*, our own clear consciences strengthen us ("...my own clear conscience strengthens me, that good companion that upholds a man within the armor of his purity." From John Ciardi's translation of *The Divine Comedy*, W. W. Norton & Company, 1961).

Maybe John Lennon can help: "Being honest may not get you a lot of friends, but it'll always get you the right ones."

My brother David states the immediate, practical reason for doing inner work now (rather than waiting) this way: "If you're working on yourself *now*, you're also improving your life *now*. When you become a better person, people respond to you better, and your life gets better." Think about what he means. If you lie habitually, you may think you're getting away with it, but most people around you know you're lying and have lost all trust and respect for you. Some will have distanced themselves; some will have completely left your life. Those more honest, more reliable people, people who would be a joy to be around and who would contribute positively to your life, are gone. What's left in your life are your fellow liars—unreliable people you can't trust and can't expect much from.

We all know when we're doing wrong. We know when we're harming others. And I believe that everyone (aside from a psychopath) feels bad for doing harm. (A study on psychopathy by Nathaniel Anderson and Kent Kiehl says that the "neurocognitive peculiarities" that characterize psychopathy "can hijack the development of our moral sensibility.")

So instead of answering your questions about why you should do inner work now, I ask you three questions.

1. Do you want to feel better about yourself?
2. Do you want to learn how to treat yourself and others better?
3. Do you want to learn and grow as a soul so you are always becoming a better being?

If you answered "yes" to any of these questions, you've answered yourself. That's your reason for becoming a better human being.

## *Ma'at's feather and the divine scales of justice*

When I was getting my second master's degree (this time in anthropology), I took a course from John Baines, a renowned Egyptologist and a guest lecturer at the University of Arizona. I chose to write my paper for the class on the meaning of Ma'at (you'll also see this spelled as Maat). Ma'at was the daughter of the creator and sun god Ra (sometimes spelled Re), and was Thoth's wife. Thoth was the god of wisdom, and given who Ma'at was and what she represented, that marriage makes complete sense. I mention Ma'at in chapter 1.

The ancient Egyptians honored Ma'at as a truthteller and the opposite of disorder; Ma'at in turn valued honest people who lived with integrity and who were true to themselves. After a human died, the Egyptians believed that our hearts (representing our souls; that is, who we had been in life) were weighed on a scale, with Ma'at's feather as the counterweight. During the weighing, the deceased needed to give 42 negative confessions, in which they addressed a specific judge and declared that they hadn't committed 42 specific crimes (theft, murder, lying, and so on). Each judge had a different domain, some on earth and some in the afterlife, and there was some overlap between the confessions.

Some people today flip these confessions and call them "ideals." For those people, although the deceased addressed judges, there was no judge as we might understand it; it was just us telling the truth about ourselves and hoping our hearts would balance against Ma'at's feather in her impartial scales. For your convenience, I've repeated figure 1 from chapter 1 here.

*Figure 30. Ma'at's scale of justice weighs a human's heart—what that human was in life—against her feather of truth. The purpose is to determine whether the human lived a life of integrity by following 42 ideals.*

In this model of weighing your heart against Ma'at's feather, if we had lived with integrity, we went to a good place. If we hadn't, Ma'at's feather wouldn't balance with our heart, and we were sent to another, less likable place. It was finally time for the chickens to come home to roost and for all our deeds to prove our worth or lack thereof. Though as I've said earlier in this book, there is no bad place; we all go to heaven. It's my opinion that Ma'at's scale and the attendant confessions represent the life review, in which we relate everything we did while in a body, and then we either are free to go to heaven proper or we must go to the special school I describe in chapter 3.

In his *Ancient Egyptian Religion: An Interpretation* (Columbia University Press, 1948), Henri Frankfort explains that Ma'at was more than justice, which is how many people in his time interpreted her meaning. He says that Ma'at belongs "as much to cosmology as to ethics. It [Ma'at] is justice as the divine order of society, but it is also the divine order of nature as established at the time of creation. In the Pyramid texts Re is said to have come from...the place of creation, 'after he had put order (Maat) in the place of chaos.'" In other words, Ma'at (truth, integrity, justice) clears up chaos. Chaos in this case means the beliefs about how things were before the Divine intervened, though it can also mean the everyday kinds of chaos that dishonesty and immorality bring.

## *Akhenaten and the belief in one god*

As I said in chapter 8, the pharaoh Akhenaten believed there was only one god, Ra, and that all the other gods, though they existed, were aspects of Ra, just as we humans living our lives are aspects of our greater souls. Some scholars speculate that Akhenaten's belief in one god was influenced by the Jews who were thought to be living in Egypt at the time. Others think it was the other way around: The Jews who, at that time, worshiped many gods, were influenced by Akhenaten to believe in only one. Either is possible, though many scholars lean toward it being the latter.

In my years of communicating with a variety of gods and goddesses and other holy beings, including the one God as I have experienced him, I have never been asked to worship any of them, or to make sacrifices to any of them, or to be afraid of them. (From the first time he contacted me, I've usually seen and communicated with God in his male aspect, though I know God is far more than a body, let alone one gender.) Instead, all divinities I've spoken with have expressed the desire that we human beings be open to developing closer relationships with them. The divinities have all been responsible and respectful, modeling the kind of relationship they wish and the kind of behavior they would like to see us humans embrace. Each has an area of human existence they are interested in. The god Loki, for example, far from being an unreliable, undesirable trickster (though he is a trickster, he is neither unreliable nor undesirable), works to help people with childhood trauma find healing.

In a later chapter in his book, Frankfort quotes from the "Teachings of Ptahhotep," an ancient Egyptian text about Ma'at that succinctly summarizes what Ma'at is about and why we should care about following her precepts. In the following quotation, I've added my explanations in square brackets. Although the text starts by addressing leaders, it applies to anyone, as the text makes clear. (I've emphasized that part in bold.)

"If thou art a leader who directs the affairs of a multitude, strive after every excellence until there be no fault in thy nature. Maat is good and its worth is lasting. It has not been disturbed since the day of its creator, whereas he who transgresses its ordinances [the ordinances of truth and integrity] is punished. **It**

**[Ma'at, truth, integrity] lies as a path in front even of him who knows nothing**. Wrongdoing has never yet brought its venture to port. It is true that evil may gain wealth, but the strength of truth is that it lasts; a man can say: 'It was the property of my father.'"

This teaching makes it clear that living in integrity is possible for anyone, even "him who knows nothing." This text also says that truth is not a physical thing, yet it's longer lasting than any material belongings. Living in integrity means being honest to ourselves and others, and being true to ourselves, both of which can be hard but aren't impossible. Lies are anathema to integrity; they interfere with our ability to be truthful and to discern truth in others. Have you noticed that dishonest people, especially people who lie to themselves, are the most distrustful of others? That's because they assume everyone is like them; that is, they believe that nobody has integrity, and no one can be trusted.

The converse is also true; honest people, people who are trustworthy, often are overly trusting and assume that others are like them. I once asked an appliance repair person if he accepted checks. He said normally not, but from me, yes, adding, "Trusting people can be trusted." He meant that people who are trusting are showing that they can be trusted.

And a final thought on truth: As shown in the stories about Ma'at, and as I mentioned earlier in this book, lies interfere with our relationship with the Divine. The Divine is complete truth; when we reject truth in our lives, we are rejecting the Divine. As Dorothy Sayers says in the introduction to her translation of Dante's *Paradise*, "The fundamental Christian proposition [is] that the journey to God is the journey into reality." (Dorothy Sayers, *The Divine Comedy 3: Paradise*, Penguin Books, 1966.) Or as Charles Williams says in many of his works, truth is the only real thing and brings us closer to the Divine and the greater Reality; lies take us further away.

## *The mountain of becoming a better human being*

As should be abundantly clear by now, I believe that one of our purposes for being here is to become better human beings. We are all on a range from not being aware there is such a thing as being a better human being, to being quite evolved and of help to everyone in the world, with most of us strung out along the line of evolving from there to here. Regardless of your beliefs, that evolutionary path of moving from unconsciousness to self and other-awareness and responsibility is that journey to the Divine.

Metatron has spoken to me about a concept that I call the mountain of becoming. That figurative mountain represents that line of evolution. It's a mountain we all climb as we become more evolved and responsible, each of us evolving at our own pace and on our own volition. The mountain is surrounded by a deep sea. The sea represents where we start.

In this analogy, we as souls all begin underwater on the sea floor. Many of us choose to stay there. Being underwater means we are unconscious and unaware. In that state of unawareness, we don't even know there is anything more than where we are, nor are we self-aware, and we don't know who we are. The sea's currents (life and life events) push us here and there and we drift with those currents. We act out our archetypes and fears without any awareness that that's what's going on. We take things literally and only see the surface of things and people; without awareness or introspection, we can't see anything more.

As long as we are underwater, unconscious and not self-aware, we aren't aware of our motivations, we aren't introspective (and we don't care that we're not, and sometimes, with the same uncomprehending lack of understanding a child might have for adult actions, we mock those who are, saying things like "You think too much" or "You're too sensitive"), and any attempt on the part of others to explain any of this makes no sense to us and doesn't reach us. Though the seeds of change are being planted by what others tell us.

At some point, we feel an impulse to move. Many ignore that impulse, choosing to remain in our comfortable place of drifting through life. We don't know what we don't know, and we don't care that we don't know. This ignorant state can be blissful.

But some of us start to pay attention. We wake up a little, become a little more self-aware, and realize we are no longer satisfied drifting through life. We want something more, but we don't know what we want or what that "more" could be. Or this change may come about in another way. Maybe something uncomfortable, either something we've done a thousand times before but are no longer happy doing, or something others around us do that they've done a thousand times before but that now suddenly disturbs us, causes us to want to move away from where we are.

So we start to move, perhaps still mostly aimlessly, but with a mild purpose: we're seeking change. And change we find. Little by little, or sometimes in a big leap, we start to move with a more focused resolve toward a greater understanding of ourselves and those around us.

Gradually the currents of the changes we make move us toward the shore, where the waves break at the foot of the mountain.

Once we reach the seashore at the foot of the mountain and our heads break above the water's surface, we start to become even more self-aware. We start to notice what's going on around us, and notice how what we do affects ourselves and others, and how what others do affect us. In the words of a long-ago professor who told me most people walk around asleep, we wake up. We may still not yet be introspective or highly self-aware—those abilities will come later, as we climb the mountain—but we have made a huge leap from walking through life oblivious and unconscious to being more aware and more conscious.

So we step out of the ocean and start ascending the mountain's slope. Little by little, step by step, as we learn more about ourselves and others, we become more aware, more caring, more discerning, more ethical, less willing to do the wrong thing and, eventually, so unwilling to do wrong that even the thought repels us.

*Figure 31. The mountain of becoming: an analogy for walking the path of becoming a better human being.*

Climbing the mountain is a metaphor for the process of becoming a better human being. The journey up the mountain is mandatory, but *when* and *how* you make that journey is under your control. You choose when to make that journey, and how much time you take on it. You might sprint up some parts of the slope, but may slow or even stop at places. You may make a quantum leap in understanding yourself and life and you may jet up the mountain. However far you've come up the mountain when you leave your bodily life determines your starting point in the afterlife.

To me, working on bettering yourself while you're in a body is paramount; a top priority; a thing to do no matter how hard it is. To others, becoming a better human being is a lower priority or not a priority at all. If you are one such, and if nothing I've said about the afterlife convinces you otherwise, that's your right. Just remember you're not avoiding anything; you're just postponing the inevitable. With this new information, can you decide now, wherever you are on that mountain, to strive to do better and to be better?

## The circle of human expression

In addition to evolving as human beings, from another perspective, we are all individuals on a circle of human expression. Those who are most like us are closest to us on the circle; we understand them best. As the circle curves away from us, we find increasingly more differences. A simple analogy is to say that if we love peppermint ice cream, those most like us may also love it or at least like it a lot. But as we look at those further away from us on the range, we find people who love different ice cream flavors. Even further away, we find people who love another dessert and don't love ice cream at all. Eventually, if we move far enough away, we find people who don't care for desserts and some who have never heard of ice cream. If you think of us as colors in a rainbow, those who are most like us are similar in color and those who are less like us are colors that are further away from us. So reds, oranges, and yellows are more similar to each other than blues and greens.

Someone being further away from us makes neither them nor us better or worse than the other. It just makes us different. We humans are like art: We might not appreciate all art, but it's enjoyable because it's an expression of someone's creative abilities. In just the same way, we might not appreciate all humans, but no matter how different they are from us, as an expression of a soul and as a human being, they are valuable. Yes, even him. And her. And whomever else you're thinking isn't worthy of life.

**The circle of human expression**

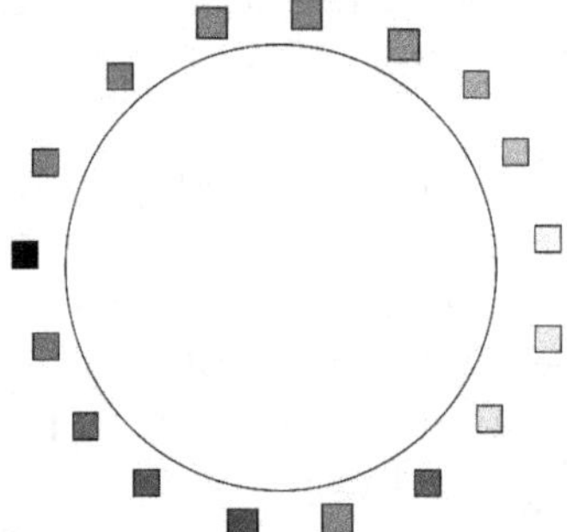

*Figure 32. The circle of human expression: We are all unique human beings.*

If you're thinking you aren't worthy, that's another matter. You could be thinking that because someone convinced you of that; you could be thinking that because you've done things you're ashamed of and believe you deserve to be punished. But that's not how Divine grace works. Punishment and the Divine don't mesh. The Divine loves everyone and forgives everyone. Forgiveness doesn't mean you can continue harming others (if that's what you've done); it means that you won't be punished for doing that harm, but will instead be responsible for improving yourself as a human being so you no longer wish to do harmful things. If you don't start that work while in a human body, you'll need to do it in the afterlife if you wish to make spiritual progress.

## *What you can do now to prepare for a more productive afterlife*

I've used the term "inner work" throughout this book; it's relevant and pertinent to the here and now and to the afterlife. The best thing we can do to prepare ourselves for life after bodily death is to do our inner work and focus more strongly on becoming a better human being now, while still in our physical bodies. Inner work involves becoming more comfortable with who we are, examining ourselves and our motivations, learning about and integrating what Carl Jung called our shadows. Most people call the part of our inner work in which we work on our shadows "shadow work." Working on our shadows means bringing into conscious awareness those aspects of ourselves we aren't acknowledging. I say more on shadow work in a bit. Even if you've heard about shadow work, unless you've studied Carl Jung, some of what I say about shadow work may surprise you.

Why do inner work now? Why not wait until the afterlife? Because this life offers unique opportunities you will never again have. Might as well do it now rather than waste this precious, one-time-only opportunity. By the time you finish reading this book, you'll understand why I say this.

Before I talk further about inner work, let's talk about fear. One of the most fundamental human fears is of being rejected and abandoned by those we love. This fear is valid and compelling, and we humans will do almost anything to avoid rejection and abandonment. (Unfortunately, this fear of rejection makes us susceptible to social engineering, in which people who wish to control us pressure us by rejecting us and expressing disapproval of our thoughts and choices.)

We therefore are often afraid to do inner work because we're afraid of discovering truths about ourselves that will make us want to reject ourselves, and will make us feel as though everyone else will reject us if they find out those things about us. If we aren't self-aware, we don't want to become self-aware for the same reasons. If we are self-aware, we might make excuses for not doing inner work, excuses that skirt the fear of abandonment. These excuses include the following:

- I don't have time.
- I don't know how to do inner work.
- I want to do my inner work "perfectly"; if I can't, then there's no reason to do it.
- Inner work is too hard.
- I don't have that much "wrong" with me, so I don't need to do any inner work.
- I'll do my inner work later in life.
- It's too late to start.
- I'll start my inner work once I'm comfortably in the afterlife.

And yet, like it or not, most other people in our lives already are abundantly aware of those things about ourselves that we are most uncomfortable with, and they haven't yet rejected or abandoned us. (Or if they have, maybe we're better off without them in our lives.) After all, nobody is perfect, and it's unrealistic and unreasonable to expect anyone, including ourselves, to be perfect.

So gather your courage and start thinking about doing inner work. Courage doesn't mean not being afraid; it means doing the right thing despite the fear. You truly have nothing to lose and everything to gain by starting your inner work now. Self-awareness is essential. Turns out that although we all have a consciousness, few of us are actually conscious and self-aware. The non-self-aware don't know what they're doing or how they're affecting others.

So the first step is to learn to be (more) self-aware. To start that process, pay attention to yourself. With every thought and action, ask yourself: What am I doing? Why am I doing it? In these ways you can learn more about yourself and become a more adult and honest person.

## *Forgiving yourself and others*

Forgiveness is important to inner work. If we are holding onto resentment, unforgiveness, and anger toward either ourselves or others, we'll have a hard time making progress toward being an evolved human being. In my book, *The Forgiving Lifestyle: How to Forgive Everyone (Including Yourself)*, (Athena Star Press, 2014), I describe a simple three-step process for forgiving yourself or others. Mind you, the forgiveness process is simple, but forgiveness isn't always easy. In the book, I address some common misconceptions about forgiveness. For example, some people refuse to forgive a person until that person recognizes they've done harm and asks for forgiveness. In some cases, that will never happen. In my book, I also explain that you aren't required to forgive anyone if you don't want to, nor do you have to forgive anyone until you are ready to do so.

## *Why do inner work?*

Why is it important to do inner work, to work on improving yourself and making yourself a better human being? I have two complementary answers, one a long-term reason and the other a practical, immediate reason.

The long-term reason is that, although you can coast through this life if you wish, and you can even coast through the afterlife, you cannot make spiritual progress if you don't work on making yourself a better soul. In the afterlife, you are encouraged in the gentlest and most loving way to work on yourself, but because of free will, you aren't required to. However, you will sit in the afterlife equivalent of limbo until you decide to start working on yourself.

Jung believed that we can all become better, more fulfilled human beings when we become aware of and fully integrate all aspects of ourselves, even those aspects we aren't comfortable with—the parts he calls our shadow. Full integration of our shadow—that is, coming to terms with our shadows—makes available to us the power and splendor of all we are, and helps strengthen us against being pressured by inner fears or outside judgment.

Jung also believed, and I agree, that unresolved shadow aspects are the primary cause of most human problems: prejudice;

conflicts, from interpersonal to group and up to the scale of wars; and other unpleasant human interactions. As Jung said, "modern people...are ignorant of what they really are. We have simply forgotten what a human being really is, so we have men like Nietzsche and Freud and Adler, who tell us what we are, quite mercilessly. We have to discover our shadow. Otherwise we are driven into a world war in order to see what beasts we are." (Carl Jung, *Visions: Notes of the Seminar Given in 1930–1934*, Princeton University Press, 1997)

Another reason to do inner work is because we are part of a community with others—family, friends, coworkers, and other human beings we come into contact with. Especially if we're a parent, we are affecting our children every minute. They watch us carefully and learn how to relate to others through the behavior and attitudes we're modeling. And we might be unconsciously inflicting trauma on them through bad parenting because of our own unresolved childhood traumas inflicted on us by our unconscious parents.

Doing our inner work therefore helps our children tremendously. It can mean not passing along generational trauma to our children. Generational trauma is trauma that a parent experienced and then passes along to their child or children, who in turn grow up and pass it along to their children, and this goes on through the generations until someone stops the pattern. Ancestral work, as I describe in chapter 10, can help stop such trauma, and so can doing inner work. And one further thought: If you've come late to inner work and your children are now adults, doing your inner work now can be unexpectedly healing for them. For example, maybe you did things to them when they were children, but never apologized to them then. It's not too late to apologize now. Sometimes that apology is all an adult child needs to start healing.

Another part of the previously mentioned passage by (possibly) Fernando Pessoa is "Being happy is to let the child living within us to live free, happy and simple. It is having the needed maturity to say 'I was wrong.' It is having the essential courage to say 'forgive me.' It is having the indispensable sensibility to say 'I need you.' It is being able to say 'I love you.' It is having the humility of receptivity."

Doing your inner work makes you a more authentic, real, honest person. Your coworkers might better appreciate working with you, and your friends may find they enjoy your company more. Your family might appreciate the changes in you. Though not always. Some people don't like it when people in their lives change. If you find people rejecting you as you become more real, that's okay—they might feel uncomfortable because you are showing that it is, after all, possible to become a better human being, and they are challenged because they didn't think it was possible, or they don't want to believe it is possible, because that would mean they have no excuse for their bad behavior. It's their choice whether they decide your self-improvement is a good thing that gives them hope, or whether they prefer to retreat into the land of denial and fear. Either way, it's not your circus and not your monkeys; that is, it's none of your business. You can rejoice if they decide to be inspired by you to themselves become better human beings, or you can mourn the end of a relationship. And you can also know that you now have room in your life for people who are more suitable for the you you're becoming.

## *What does it mean to do inner work?*

Inner work doesn't mean working on tolerating the things others do that annoy us; instead, it means focusing on ourselves, learning who we really are and what motivates us, and working on changing those things about ourselves that we want to improve.

Many people think that inner work is only about working on our shadows. Our shadows are those things about ourselves that we aren't acknowledging to ourselves. But inner work isn't just shadow work; it's also consciously addressing those parts of ourselves that are causing us or others distress, parts that we're aware of but have hitherto been choosing to continue doing despite the effect on ourselves or others.

Here's an example of an inner work project I undertook years ago. In the 1980s, I started studying the Myers-Briggs Typology Indicator (MBTI), a personality assessment tool based on Carl Jung's theories of temperament (Which were in turn based on ancient Greek ideas.) I learned that some traits about myself that I had always assumed everyone had were not, in fact, universal.

One of those traits was that, as a highly intuitive and introverted person, I assumed everyone around me noticed what was going on with other people without anyone having to say anything.

So, for example, I would mentally appreciate a person and assumed they knew I appreciated them. This turned out not to be the case. In retrospect, it makes sense. Many people aren't good at reading people, let alone mind readers, so how was anyone supposed to know I appreciated them if I didn't say it aloud?

For extroverts, the opposite is true: They blurt out whatever's on their mind without thinking whether what they are thinking needs to be said, let alone whether how they say it could be tempered by kindness.

As someone always striving to become a better person, knowing this about myself—that I was leaving unsaid a lot of things that should be said—I decided to work on expressing myself verbally. This was and still is hard for me. I've spent decades teaching myself to speak up for myself and to express appreciation of and to others.

But I've made immense progress, and others have commented on the improvement. It's gratifying that others see the difference, and also a little bit embarrassing, because it means others noticed that flaw and politely chose to say nothing. Which emphasizes a point I made earlier: Others in your life almost certainly know your flaws better than you do, so you might as well start fixing them. I feel better about myself for having taken responsibility for an unattractive character trait and successfully transforming it. Even though I haven't been completely successful in changing this habit, I've made good progress, and others, I presume, feel more relaxed around me because they don't have to guess what I'm thinking. That's important to remember: When doing inner work, your success lies in whether you've improved *enough*, not in whether you've been 100 percent successful.

## *Maslow's hierarchy of self-actualization*

One thing to know about improving yourself is that it's easier to do when your needs are met. Abraham Maslow, an American humanist psychologist and follower of Jung, wrote about what he called our hierarchy of needs. When I studied this theory, the needs were presented as a ladder, called Maslow's hierarchy of self-actualization, with our most basic needs on the bottom. Initially this hierarchy was represented by a ladder. Later representations show it as a series of layers or a pyramid, again with the bottom layer being our most basic needs and the subsequent layers containing needs that Maslow called our higher needs. The needs are as follows, from bottom to top.

1. Physical survival (food, shelter, clothing)
2. Safety (physical, financial, and emotional)
3. Belonging and love (friendship and family)
4. Esteem (self-esteem, self-respect, respect from others)
5. Cognitive needs (creativity, curiosity, morality, problem-solving, acceptance of what is)
6. Aesthetic needs (the ability to appreciate life and beauty, appreciating nature)

Maslow later added another top layer, transcendence (spiritual needs). Maslow said we must have our most basic needs met before we can be interested in working on the higher ones. He argued that if you are struggling to survive, you won't have the mental or emotional resources to worry about anything further.

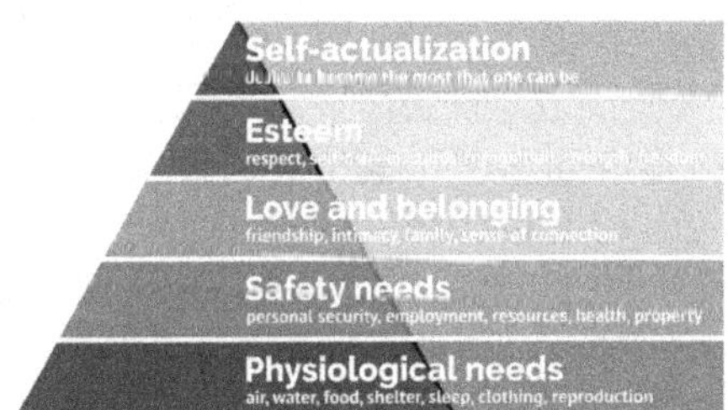


Maslow's hierarchy of needs

*Figure 33. Maslow's ladder of self-actualization is a tiered list of things we need in life, starting with the most basic and rising to the need for transcendence.*

Maslow's hierarchy can be useful, though I disagree with his premise that we can't work on higher needs when our lower needs are unfulfilled. Like Phila (remember the story I recounted in chapter 4 from the Tutu's book?), we all have the capacity to be moral even when our lives are threatened, and no matter where we are in terms of having our needs met, we can still decide to make ourselves better human beings. I look at Maslow's hierarchy as a useful tool for checking in on yourself while you do inner work: Are you making sure you're getting your needs met? Are you overdoing some aspect of your inner work at the cost of ignoring your needs? For example, are you ignoring your need for sleep so you can read a good book?

## *The scariness of doing inner work*

As I said earlier, inner work is scary. It brings us closer to seeing reality as it is and not as we wish it were. It raises fears. As I mentioned earlier, one of our biggest fears is of being cast out from the community. We are all afraid of rejection and abandonment, and starting on inner work brings those fears to the fore, consciously or unconsciously, in a big, almost inconfrontable way. Fear should never be underestimated. Our fears will drive us forever until we face them. Fear drives many people to do the unthinkable to themselves or each other, or to avoid doing what needs to be done. ("If I do the right thing, what will others think? Will I survive?")

One of the biggest tasks of doing inner work is accepting responsibility for ourselves and rejecting the temptation to play the victim. When we play the victim, we pretend we are powerless, retreating behind the lie that we have no agency and no control over ourselves; that instead others are "making us" feel, say, or do things. When we believe we're a victim, we feel sorry for ourselves. We blame others and believe we have nothing to apologize for or make amends for; after all, why should we apologize or make amends for something we had no hand in doing? We hold frequent pity parties, and if asked for an apology, we never apologize. Instead we give non-apologies like "I'm sorry you feel that way," which blames the person we're "apologizing" to, or we say things like "I'm sorry you think I did anything wrong," which essentially tells the person we're "apologizing" to that we think they're at fault. Such false apologies further the damage we've already done.

If we're deeply committed to being a victim, we might even completely forget memories of having done harmful things, and we might make up new, more positive memories in which we were the hero. Believing that we are a victim can be our response to abuse, including childhood abuse and trauma, and we don't want to revisit those experiences. So we can choose to avoid examining ourselves because we're afraid of facing the pain, fear, betrayal, and abandonment we felt in our childhood.

But nothing will change if we don't face those fears. We're adults now and are often no longer under the thumb of our abusers. Or if we are still under their thumbs, it's time to admit that we are and walk away. Once we face our fears, usually two things happen: We find out we have more courage than we thought we had, and often, the thing we feared shrinks to something manageable, making it easier for us to deal with what we fear, and to continue on our path. The mountain we feared becomes a navigable molehill, something we can simply step over or around.

## *Inner work is only mandatory if we want to evolve*

As I said earlier, though inner work makes us better human beings and improves our lives, that work isn't mandatory while we live in a physical body; it is only mandatory in the afterlife if we want to evolve as a soul. Though even then, although it's mandatory if we want to progress, we get to choose when we start that work. So why do it now? Jung gives a succinct reason: "Until you make the unconscious conscious, it will direct your life and you will call it fate." Or you may continue to act like a victim and play mind games with people around you, unaware that you're playing those games and unaware of how your game-playing is affecting others. You'll figure it out in the afterlife, but wouldn't you rather figure it out now?

Inner work is hard, sometimes in unexpected ways. As you evolve and become a better human being, you may find yourself losing friends, either because they leave you or you leave them, because you and your friends are no longer in the same place. You may find yourself walking away from people, places, and situations because you are no longer comfortable with those people, places, and situations, or you may find that, for your own survival, you must walk away from those people, places, and situations because they present a danger to you. A good analogy for this kind of action is that of the drug user who gets clean and distances themselves from their former friends who are still using drugs. The drug user knows that being around such people will give them too many opportunities to use, possibly ending in an overdose and death.

Yet you will also find people moving into your life who are more in alignment with the newer, more ethical, more honest, kinder, gentler, more compassionate, and more empathetic you.

While in a physical body, we can remain in denial and not do any inner work. We feel we are somehow safe from the immensity and power of the Real as long as we pretend it doesn't exist. And there's some truth to that. If you don't stare into the abyss, it won't notice you. As Friedrich Nietzsche said: "[I]f you gaze for long into an abyss, the abyss gazes also into you." (*Beyond Good and Evil: Prelude to a Philosophy of the Future*, chapter IV, "Apothegms and Interludes," paragraph 146. C. G. Naumann of Leipzig, 1886).

*Figure 34. Inner work can be scary. When we gaze into the abyss, the abyss looks back at us. Inner work can also be rewarding when we find that things we feared aren't so frightening after all.*

But once we come out of the complaisance of denial and start to confront who we are, we see a tiny crack through which we glimpse the Real. It can seem like an abyss. It can terrify us, send us scurrying back to the safety of mental darkness. Or it can challenge us to continue the work, imperfectly though we may be doing it, refining our dross like an alchemist until the Real becomes, perhaps no less terrifying, but also comforting and welcoming. Eventually we come to prefer the uncomfortable Real to our previous comfortable blindness.

Think of what a relief it will be to you and others around you when you decide to start working on yourself. Especially, if you've been habitually dishonest, think how much better it will be for everyone. It's better for you because you'll be free of the tension that lying brings, and life will start coming into a sharper, more real focus. It's better for others because they can stop discounting everything you say and can start trusting you. (If it isn't too late, and if they haven't already distanced themselves from you entirely because of your constant dishonesty.)

Here's a story of how we seldom get away with dishonesty, even when we think our lies are undetected. I befriended a young woman, I'll call her Leslie, who lied habitually. Because she was young and I liked her and had hope for her, I tolerated her dishonesty, but gently let her know each time she lied that I knew she was lying. (I'm not claiming any great perceptive ability; her lies were clumsy and obvious.) After discussing her dishonesty with her several times, warning her that I don't tolerate that level of dishonesty in my close relationships, I finally told her I was ending the friendship because she continued lying. Her telling response was, "But I've never lied to *you*," which was a lie in itself, because she had frequently lied to me. Her response showed me she was aware she lied regularly, but she didn't want to change.

I told my late friend Steve about this person, and he said he used to be like Leslie: He lied all the time, with no reason to lie. A drill sergeant finally called him on his lies, and that was Steve's first intimation that he wasn't getting away with lying. He reflected on his life and realized that many beloved former friends, people who were honest and had integrity, people who had eased themselves out of his life, had almost certainly distanced themselves because of his lying; they just hadn't cared enough for the friendship to do the really hard thing of confronting him. At the time of losing those friendships, he didn't think there was a connection to anything he'd done; he thought the friendships had just naturally ended. He said the wake-up call from the drill sergeant cut him deeply and caused him to choose to change. Yet despite how hard it was for Steve to realize that about himself, he felt a whole lot better about himself as he worked on changing.

The irony is that the more honest a person is, the more trusting they are, and yet the more easily they spot another person's lies. Sometimes it takes a while, but they always figure it out. If you habitually lie, you may think you're getting away with it (and almost certainly the first person you're lying hardest to is yourself). But you aren't getting away with it, and your life is poorer because of it.

If you're wondering why I keep using lying as an example, it's because so many people lie regularly. Sometimes they call their lies "white lies," thinking that those lies are somehow okay. But as Charles Williams, a Christian mystic who was a close friend of J.R.R. Tolkien and C.S. Lewis, says in so many of his books, you are closer to the Divine (Reality) when you see, accept, and state the truth, and you move further away from the Divine when you reject the truth and tell lies. As Saint Teresa of Ávila said about the devil (and by extension, all demonic forces), "He is a friend of lies, and the lie himself. He will make no pact with anyone who walks in truth." However you want to interpret the devil, as either a being or a way of being, her words caution us all to be rigorously honest lest we fall into bad company.

## *Does inner work fix everything?*

Doing inner work doesn't mean you instantly "fix" everything about yourself. And it doesn't mean you completely, 100 percent fix something specific about yourself. It does mean that you are starting to improve.

Just as my friend Steve found, doing inner work is hard and uncomfortable, but it feels satisfying, like using muscles that have atrophied and that you are now rehabilitating. And ponder this: Truth and the Divine are inextricably interrelated. To embrace the truth is to embrace the Divine; to reject the truth is to reject the Divine.

Sometimes inner work means facing the trauma others have inflicted on you. Trauma is complicated; if you know or suspect you've experienced trauma, I recommend seeing a counselor or faith leader. Sometimes we find we don't want to talk about our traumatic experiences because of misplaced loyalty: we are protecting those who harmed us. But as Anne Lamott once said, "You own everything that happened to you. Tell your stories. If people wanted you to write warmly about them, they should have behaved better."

Behaving better doesn't mean behaving perfectly all the time. It means owning up to our mistakes, apologizing, making amends, and learning how to do better the next time. It takes strength and courage to be honest, and a sense of ethics and a commitment to doing the right thing. Those things are the minimum requirements for being a decent human being. You may feel you don't have those traits, or that you aren't strong enough to develop them, but every time you do the right thing, you're getting stronger. And hard as it is to own up; it's much harder to let someone suffer because you don't fess up. Maybe you don't think so, but that just means you are out of touch with your basic humanity.

If someone can't be honest and responsible, which also means being accountable for their actions, they have inner work to do. By being accountable, I mean that when Person A approaches Person B and says "What you did hurt me," the responsible and mature action for person B to do is to say "I'm sorry" and to strive to be better. It would be irresponsible and harmful for Person B to deny they did anything, or to give a false apology like those I discussed earlier. It's fine for Person B to be imperfect and be where they are on their path, but as Jesus once told me, we don't have to hang out with souls who aren't responsible. If someone is harming you and they won't stop, or if they harmed you but won't accept accountability for it, you can leave them.

I say that knowing it's complicated. Sometimes family members harm other family members and then never accept accountability for their actions. If you try to talk with them about it, even if all you want is an apology, those family members might do what's called DARVO. DARVO stands for deny, attack, and reverse victim and offender. In short, they deny they ever did the harmful thing, attack you instead, and play the victim, saying *you* were the one to harm *them*. If someone DARVOs you, chances are they will never, ever apologize or admit to any wrong-doing.

In such cases, especially with family, it can be super hard to distance yourself from them. If the abuse is in the past and you are handling the effects through counseling, you may need to accept that you will never get the apology you need, and you then get to decide whether to keep that person in your life (if they are still in your life). But if the abuse is ongoing, it is unlikely it will ever stop, so you need to decide your next step, which may be distancing yourself (going low contact) or cutting that person out of your life entirely.

And if you're the one DARVOing others, ask yourself (assuming you're aware enough to know you're doing it), why you do it. What are you afraid of? Why can't you admit you did something harmful to someone you love? Why do you play the victim instead of accepting responsibility and accountability? The answers to those questions can help you, maybe even lead you to the wisdom you need to stop doing such things. I say that while recognizing that some people, such as narcissists, disassociate themselves from their bad acts and no longer remember doing those harmful things (because of narcissistic amnesia). When confronted, they genuinely don't remember doing anything harmful. If you find to your bewilderment that many people accuse you of doing the same kinds of harmful things, things you don't remember, that can be an indication that something in yourself needs addressing.

## *An overview of shadow work*

After reading this preliminary discussion on shadow work, you may be interested in starting it. (If you're not, you can skip to the last section in this chapter.)

We all have traits we would rather not own as being true about ourselves. As Alice Miller says in the revised edition of her book, *The Drama of the Gifted Child* (Basic Books, 1997), "At first it will be mortifying to see that [we are] not always good, understanding, tolerant, controlled, and, above all, without needs, for these have been the basis of [our] self-respect." She also says that we are free "only when self-esteem is based on the authenticity of one's own feelings and not on the possession of certain qualities."

Although I learned much from Alice Miller's book, her son, Martin Miller, says in his book, *The True "Drama of the Gifted Child"* (independently published, 2018) that Alice Miller never confronted her own trauma from surviving the Holocaust. As a result, she was a terrible mother, inflicting her trauma on her son. Martin Miller says his mother may even have helped the Nazis find Jews to kill, and even more horrifically, almost certainly married one of the Nazis she helped, Martin Miller's abusive father.

If you read Alice Miller's book, keep in mind that perhaps some of the vaguer portions in her book are from her not confronting her own trauma, and therefore from her not being able to go deeply into some subjects.

I believe Martin Miller. So many of our teachers pass along their unresolved trauma to their families or followers. It takes a lot of discernment to spot the imperfections in our teachers. It also means deciding whether our teachers must be 100 percent perfect for us to learn from them. That's impossible. None of us are perfect. Instead we must decide what kinds of imperfections are acceptable and which are unacceptable. Some kinds of imperfection, such as ego or arrogance and the like, might be acceptable; others, such as abuse, prejudice, a lack of integrity (if your leader lacks integrity, how can you trust anything they say?), or otherwise doing harm, are unacceptable. Learn what you can from such people, whether their flaw are acceptable or unacceptable, and walk away when you need to.

Before Alice Miller, psychotherapists believed that the parents were always right, and if a child had a complaint, that was a fault in the child and had nothing to do with how they were raised. This attitude did an enormous amount of damage, especially because psychologists are persons in authority. Alice Miller's biggest contribution to the field of psychology was that she was the first to take the child's point of view and experiences into consideration in psychotherapy, saying (ironically) that the parent wasn't always right, and sometimes the child was telling the truth about parental misdeeds. Martin Miller agrees with the value of that part of her work.

Martin Miller disagrees with his mother's recommendation that adults confront their parents with their crimes. As has been validated by many other therapists, he says that confronting abusive parents won't work and can often lead to further harm. Instead, he recommends that people learn to confront their internalized parents and work out the relationships that way, preferably with the help of a good counselor or faith leader. An internalized parent is an image in your mind of what your parent was like and sometimes what you think a parent should be like. That's not always a good thing. If your internalized parent is abusive, unless you resolve that, you're going to think all parents are and should be abusive, and you'll be abusive too once you become a parent. Or if your internalized parent is a saint because that's how you saw your real parent, but in fact your real parent had been abusive or was at least imperfect (which they had to have been, because nobody's perfect), you almost certainly are in denial about some things you need to address in yourself.

To do our shadow work, we start noticing those things about ourselves that are on the edge of our awareness. We question every belief we have about ourselves, asking if it's true.

## *What the shadow is*

When Alice Miller speaks of us being mortified to find things are true about us that we don't like, she's talking about our shadows. Most people have heard of Carl Jung's theory of our shadows—those parts of ourselves that we don't want to acknowledge are true about us. We might not want to admit to ourselves that we can be selfish, or cruel, or prejudiced, or misogynist. These are examples; the exact things we don't want to acknowledge as true about ourselves vary from person to person.

Why would we want to acknowledge unpleasant things about ourselves? Why can't we just stay in denial about our shadow aspects? If there are things about ourselves we don't want to know, what harm is there in leaving those things undiscovered?

Because, Jung said, for wholeness, and to make the world a better, more peaceful place, we need to clearly see and integrate our shadow aspects, so that there's nothing about us that we are in denial about. When we are in denial about some aspect of ourselves, we don't see ourselves clearly, which means we can't do anything about our actions arising out of those aspects of ourselves that we are in denial about. Let's say that someone has a cruel streak and sometimes does cruel things to other people, or to animals. If they are in denial about that cruel streak, and instead like to think of themselves as a good person who wouldn't harm a fly, they won't admit their cruel actions to themselves, let alone to others. If someone else tries to discuss their cruel actions with them, they'll deny it and accuse the other person of lying. Unless they are on a path of self-discovery and honesty and are willing to at least entertain the idea that perhaps some things they do are cruel, they will continue being cruel. But not forever. Once in their life review, relating every action they did in physical life, they can then start healing whatever caused that cruel streak.

Truth is a strength, a rock upon which we can stand. Denial, a form of lying, is a floor of sand that can be washed away at any time. When we deny something; that is, when we lie to ourselves or others about something, we close our eyes to a truth about reality. The more we close our eyes to reality, the less we can see truth (and reality) and the easier it becomes to ignore truth (and reality). And the easier it is to likewise be fooled by others into believing their lies and not perceiving that they are lying. Taken too far, we see barely anything of reality, and instead see a movie playing inside our head. But we think the movie is reality and respond to the movie, making our actions increasingly less congruent with what's going on around us.

The converse is true as well. The more truthful we are to others and ourselves, the more we can see what is true; we see reality as it is and not as we wish it to be. Sometimes that reality isn't wonderful, but it is real nonetheless, and therefore more precious than any false fantasy. When we develop the habit of honesty, we eventually become unable to tell a lie without suffering agonies of shame. And we start to feel more stable and secure in the world because we are being true to ourselves. People around us trust us more, and we'll have authentic relationships.

Being honest also enhances our ability to discern lies on all fronts, from personal to political. As Hannah Arendt, a German-American historian and philosopher, said, "If everybody always lies to you, the consequence is not that you believe the lies, but rather that nobody believes anything any longer." Arendt was speaking in the context of politics, but the statement is equally applicable to our everyday personal lives. Taking that approach, what she means is what I've said a few times throughout this book: When you're used to lying to both yourself and others, you lose the plot and can no longer see the truth in either yourself or others.

We can use a habit of honesty to integrate our shadows. Integrating our shadows requires truth. By being honest with ourselves, we can allow ourselves to see aspects of ourselves that are in our shadow and that we can now accept. Integration gives us a strength that helps us stand against people who want to tear us down. (Unfortunately, such people exist; they might be jealous or wish to control us.) Being honest also helps us to be confident enough to do what we feel called to do; to stand up for what's right in ourselves and others; to comfortably disagree with others without feeling we must attack them.

Another reason to do our shadow work is because if we are in denial about a personal characteristic, we may project that characteristic onto others. Projection is, alas, more common than I'd like to think; it arises out of unconsciousness and a lack of self-awareness.

## *What is projection?*

Projection is the process of

1. Taking something that is true about yourself,
2. denying to yourself that it is true about yourself, and then instead
3. saying that it's true about someone else.

Let's go into this a bit more. Let's say you're telling lies about someone, but you don't let yourself see that you're lying. You want to think you're completely honest and that you don't tear others down behind their backs. So you deny to yourself that you lie and instead accuse someone else of telling lies about you; very likely, you accuse the person about whom you are telling lies. Or maybe if you're a big-time liar, you accuse everyone around you of lying.

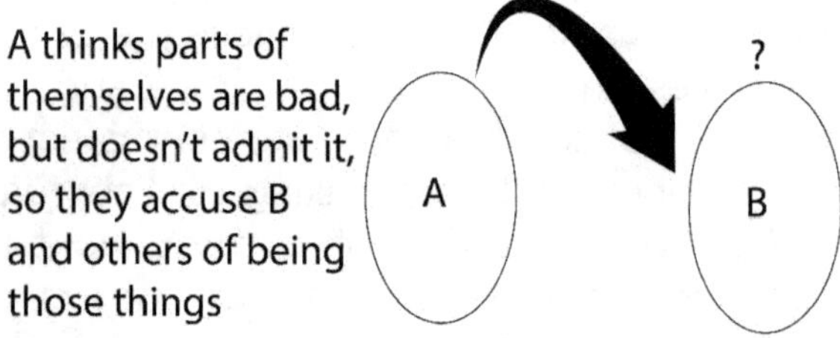


*Figure 35. The process of projection. We take something that's true about ourselves, deny it, and see it in others instead. Though we normally project bad things onto others, we can also deny good things about ourselves and instead project them onto others.*

Or let's say you're envious of an artist friend. Rather than facing the unpleasant fact that you're envious, you verbally tear down your friend where they are most talented, telling them that they're not talented, sabotaging them by suggesting ways for them to change their creative works in a way that destroys what's best and most unique about their art, and telling them, "I'm just trying to help you." Such actions are a form of gaslighting. Gaslighting is the process of saying and doing invalidating things to undermine a person's self-confidence. Gaslighters have deep, deep issues, usually involving wanting to always be in control of everyone and everything around them. If someone habitually gaslights you, don't confront them. Just walk away. They aren't going to change; confronting them only gives them more chances to gaslight you. If you don't think you can walk away from the gaslighter, see a counselor or faith leader.

If you are in denial about what you see as an unattractive personal trait of yours, and are projecting it onto others, you won't see the damage you are doing, not just to those around you, but to yourself.

There's a difference between projection and seeing what's true about someone. Let's take the lying example. If instead of thinking that everyone is lying, you notice that just one of your acquaintances lies a lot, that's highly unlikely to be projection. Instead, it's an observation.

You can get a clue about your shadow from your projections, even before you realize they're projections. For example, if you notice that you think everyone around you is selfish, you can remind yourself that it's just not possible that everyone is selfish. More likely, you are projecting a selfish aspect of yourself onto others. When you recognize that, ask yourself in what ways you are selfish. Or if you're "sure" you're honest, but you are suspicious of everyone else and are sure everyone is lying all the time, chances are you lie a lot, especially to yourself. The thing to do is not to criticize yourself or to wallow in being a victim, because that's not useful in shadow work. Instead, ask yourself questions about your motives and actions so you can pull those aspects of yourself into the light to examine and come to terms with.

Also, and this is important: **our shadows are traits we aren't acknowledging about ourselves**. Those traits aren't all bad; they can also be good traits. We can project what's good about ourselves onto others, not seeing that those good things are a truth about ourselves. If you are habitually a kind person, but was convinced by your parents that you were the opposite, you may often see others as kind, and think you aren't, instead of recognizing that the kindness is a truth about yourself.

## *Our bodies and our shadows*

Our bodies are affected by our shadows. Attacking ourselves for how we look, feeling that we or others are somehow unacceptable or "less than" if we don't meet a narrow standard of beauty and appearance—those are some ways in which our shadows manifest. Our shadows and the work required to bring them into the light can be complicated by trauma and abuse. Our bodies give us clues about our shadows and our trauma. If you want to investigate how your body might be telling you things you need to know about yourself, I recommend Bessel van der Kolk's *The Body Keeps the Score: Brain, Mind, and Body in the Healing of Trauma* (Penguin Books, 2014). The author's premise is that the trauma we experience is stored in our bodies and manifests as physical ailments and restrictions, a premise that many, many researchers have confirmed.

## *Shadow work isn't easy, even though Jung says it is*

Jung never said shadow work is easy; instead, he said, "One does not become enlightened by imagining figures of light, but by making the darkness conscious. The latter procedure, however, is disagreeable and therefore not popular." True words indeed. Not only does one not walk into the gates of Mordor, no one *wants* to. Shadow work, inner work, is hard and often cringe-inducing. But the personal and global rewards are immeasurable. Though Jung does say that it's relatively easy to see our shadows, so there's that. (Carl Jung, *Aion: Researches into the Phenomenology of the Self*, second edition, Princeton University Press, 1979.)

I'm not a counselor, nor am I an expert in shadow work, though I've done a lot of my own, and I can point you in the direction of techniques you can use and resources where you can start (or continue) your shadow work. The most important trait to bring to this work is honesty: honesty to yourself and honesty to others, no matter what. The only case in which lying is okay is if you need to lie to save your own or someone else's life. Nothing else is important enough to compromise your soul by lying.

If you struggle with shadow and inner work, consult with a counselor or faith leader to see what they can do to help you. If you feel you are particularly fragile, I strongly recommend seeking a counselor or faith leader. Remember that counselors and faith leaders are people and none of them are perfect; some will be more skilled at what you need than others, and some will be more compatible with you. Counselors and faith leaders can have shadows too, and some of them might not understand what shadow work is or agree it's valuable. Keep looking if you don't like the first counselor or faith leader you consult. Bear in mind the best counselor won't tell you there's nothing to work on, nor will they make conclusions for you; instead, they'll gently guide you toward seeing yourself more clearly.

## *Our shadows aren't all bad things*

Most people think that our shadow aspects are all bad things —the cowardly, critical, dishonest, selfish, greedy, irresponsible, harm-doing, and other such parts of our being, the parts we cringe from and don't want to think are true of us. Yet as I said earlier, Jung didn't say the shadow is all bad. It's usually a surprise to people when I tell them that Jung said the shadow is those parts *we don't want to acknowledge are true about us*. Jung said in *Aion* that the shadow "does not consist only of morally reprehensible tendencies, but also displays a number of good qualities, such as normal instincts, appropriate reactions, realistic insights, creative impulses, etc."

What does that mean? It means that if we were raised in an abusive household, we were taught that we were unacceptable human beings. Out of self-defense, we believed the lies our parents screamed at us with murder in their eyes. We came to believe we were stupid, always wrong, clumsy, selfish, crazy, and so on—all the things that were true about our parents that they were projecting onto us.

Guess what? For most of us, none of those things are true. Instead, if this happened to you, you are likely an empathetic, kind, caring, loving being who is finely tuned to the needs of others.

Yet because of your parent's projecting onto you, you don't believe those good things about yourself, and because you don't believe those good things about yourself, those traits have become part of your shadow. When raised like this, it can be surprisingly difficult to accept good things about ourselves, and we can think we're being selfish when we are simply taking our turn or setting healthy boundaries. We've introjected our parent's attacks.

## *Introjection is the opposite of projection*

What is introjection? Introjection is the opposite of projection. With projection, we take something that's true about ourselves, deny it, and see that trait in other people. With introjection, we take what somebody else believes about us and decide it's true about ourself. We deny that the opposite is true about us. Like projection, introjection isn't conscious; instead, it's something children often do as a defense when abused emotionally. They say to themselves, "Mommy says I'm stupid; I must be stupid. Mommy says I'm selfish; I must be selfish. For Mommy to love me, I must agree with her." Then they forget that they made that decision, and thereafter, the child believes those are truths about themselves, and they continue to believe those things well into adulthood, and throughout their lives if they never address the trauma or do any inner work, including shadow work. The truth is right in front of us, but we're blind to it. This process of taking the parent's point of view is reinforced by the strong loyalty children feel toward their parents, and their strong desire to please their parents.

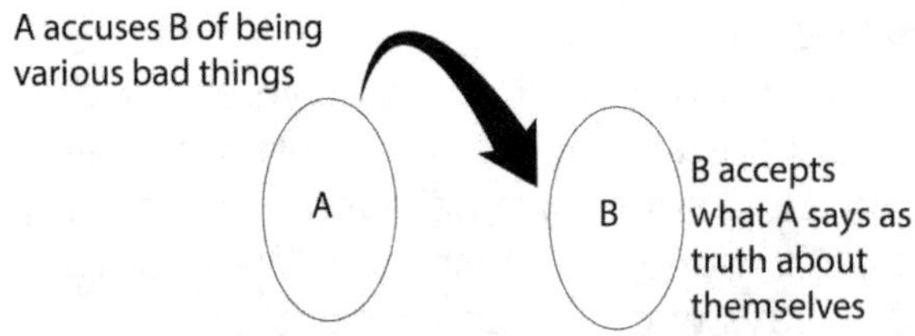


*Figure 36. The process of introjection. We take what's said about us as a truth about ourselves.*

With introjection, you still have a shadow, but the shadow now contains all the good things about yourself that you were browbeaten into not believing about yourself.

We often find projection paired with introjection. With introjection, we project our goodness onto others, often seeing something that isn't there. We may, for example, think someone is admirably honest and ethical, when in fact it is our own honesty and ethics we are projecting onto others. We might not be seeing the other person clearly; they may be dishonest and lack ethics, but we don't realize we're projecting our shadow onto them. In that way we are often fooled and taken advantage of, and end up blaming ourselves when we realize we've been bamboozled by a person who most decidedly was none of the good things we saw in them. Until we start our shadow work, and come to realize that we've been projecting our own goodness onto others, we'll continue to fall prey to the unscrupulous.

## *Learning to be a better human being*

You are unique, and your life and your journey are your own. Therefore I can only give a high-level overview of how to start or continue your journey of self-improvement, of becoming a better human being, of becoming more self-aware and self-correcting.

If you're interested in learning about the shadow and shadow work, Carl Jung originated the idea, but his works, although useful, are quite difficult. You can find many, many popular resources—books, videos, websites—dedicated to shadow work and toward the self-examined life and so on; however, there's a lot of unfiltered dross on the internet. Just be aware that, as is often the case in other fields, many laypeople who teach shadow work don't understand it. For example, many people teaching shadow work teach that the shadow is all bad, which you now know isn't so.

Possibly the best place to go is to find a trusted guide who has walked the path of self-examination and self-discovery long enough to know how to help you start or continue on that path. Though if you're far enough along on your path, you may not need a guide, and you may have already developed enough discernment to sort through the available resources and decide what's best for you.

## *It's never too late to change your mind, even after bodily death*

For people in the special school, it's too late to change their earthly choices. Their physical bodies are dead, so the ship of being a better person in physical life has sailed. But it's not too late for them to choose to start learning how to be a better being for what comes next for them, and in fact they *can't* move on to what comes next until they become a better being.

Since you're reading this book, you're still in a physical body. (Or so I assume; it's possible nonphysical entities can read human books.) Therefore it's not too late for you to start (or continue) to improve yourself before you leave your earthly body. If you're still reluctant to start, ask yourself some questions. Are you worried you might be too late, or that you have so much work to do, you'll never finish it, or that you can't do the work? Or that you're too old? Or maybe you've been doing your inner work, but fear you won't finish it in time? None of those are good excuses. It's never too late, even if you were to start your inner work a day before you died.

The parable of the workers in the vineyard in the Christian Bible (Matthew 20:1-16) illustrates this situation. In the parable, a vineyard owner hires workers at the start of the day, promising them each a denarius (a day's wage). They agree and get to work. Later in the day, the owner hires more workers and says he'll pay them "whatever is right." He does this a few more times throughout the day, hiring his last batch of workers at 5 in the afternoon. (The vineyard owner's question to that last batch of workers when hiring them is pertinent: "Why do you stand here idle all the day?" he asks. The workers respond, "Because no one has hired us.")

When pay time comes, the workers who arrived last are paid first, each receiving a denarius. Seeing this, the workers who worked longer expect more, but everyone is paid the same wage. The longer-working workers complain, but the vineyard owner says he was paying them according to their agreement, and that it is his right to pay others what he wants to pay them.

When I first heard this story, I sided with the complaining workers. Surely someone who worked more hours deserved more pay than those who came late to the work!

But now I see this story as an illustration of that infinite justice and mercy in the afterlife that I've mentioned a few times. Why shouldn't someone be rewarded fairly for doing the work, however much they completed? If they were willing to do the work for "whatever was fair," and the vineyard owner decides a full day's wage is fair for those who worked fewer hours, is that not an act of generosity on the vineyard owner's part, and a reward for the worker's willingness? If someone waits to be called to do their inner work, and they are called late, what's important is that they answer the call; they're rewarded just the same.

And indeed, the parable begins by saying the kingdom of heaven is like the vineyard's owner. The later workers' statement that they are idle because no one has hired them can be interpreted to mean that no one has called them to do their inner work, but now that the vineyard owner has called them, they set to the (inner) work willingly.

As *A Course in Miracles* (ACIM) says, a little willingness is all that's needed, and the Divine will come the rest of the way to meet us. ACIM says "Trust not your good intentions. They are not enough. But trust implicitly your willingness, whatever else may enter." (ACIM, chapter 18: IV.) The parable of the vineyard is another version of that message of the Divine coming the rest of the way to us.

ACIM (Foundation for Inner Peace, 1976) is a text received from Jesus by Helen Schucman, a Jewish psychologist. It's about forgiveness and hope and viewing a perfected world; about how we all have God's love and help. I highly recommend ACIM. But only if you read it yourself, and not read what others tell you it means. (By that I mean not blindly believing anyone's interpretations. Make up your mind about whether you agree with anyone else until after you've read ACIM.) I say this because as with any holy writing, people have crept on the scene who misunderstand ACIM's message, but think (or claim they think) they understand it, and present their misunderstandings as truth. So you'll find corrupted interpretations. It's always best to read source materials and think what they mean for you rather than let anyone else tell you what to think of them.

## *Beginning your inner work*

It's not my place to tell you where, when, or how to begin inner work, though I encourage you to consider doing the work and starting it now. You'll be ahead by however much inner work you can complete before you get to the afterlife. If you're open to and willing to do the work, the needed resources will come your way. Having said that, I'll recommend some places to start. Let your heart and soul lead you to what will do you the most good. I recommend you find something that's fun for you. It's much easier to learn and change when you're enjoying some aspect of the process.

Reading, writing in a journal, expressive art (using art as a way to express yourself, not as a competitive sport), self-awareness classes, counseling, YouTube videos, cathartic (but not traumatizing) movies, physical movement—all these things can help you learn more about yourself. In the following paragraphs, I give a few specific suggestions.

You can go the intellectual, rational route through consulting a counselor or faith leader, reading, taking classes, and so on. Or you can go the route of spirituality and the arts. Or the route of physicality—exercise, yoga, hiking, walking, and so on. Or you can combine the approaches.

One easy, gentle way to start inner work is to read (or listen to) Wayne Dyer's *Pulling Your Own Strings* (Funk & Wagnalls Co, 1978). The book has been around for decades, reprinted many times, and deservedly so. Dyer teaches that, rather than focus on what other people are doing wrong to you, you have more agency by focusing on learning to be more responsible for yourself.

Joseph Campbell's *Hero with a Thousand Faces* (Pantheon Press, 1949) talks about the power of myth and legends and how they resonate within us today. In my first introduction to inner work in a class when attending Santa Clara University, we students read this book, then were invited to write our own fairy tale. The results were illuminating—it was a way to learn truths about ourselves even though we thought we were just making things up, though it took me years to understand what my fairy tale was telling me about myself. If you decide to write your own fair tale, be aware that sometimes the meaning of our fairy tales isn't at first obvious to us, though it can be to those who know us. Or we might take years to understand what we were trying to tell ourselves as we unpeel layers and years of fear and denial.

Your fairy tale can reveal your life script—an unconscious set of beliefs and actions, decided in your childhood, that you live by until you make them more conscious through inner work. Eric Berne describes life scripts in his book, *What Do You Say After You Say Hello?* (Grove Press, 1969). Although quite old, that book has many insights that are still valid today. (But be aware the book is quite densely written and hard to get through.) According to Berne, our scripts are based on us seeking approval from our parents, especially our mothers. But what if our mothers couldn't be pleased? Berne says many life problems ensue, ranging from accepting her disapproval and forever proving her right by failing repeatedly, to rejecting our need for love and approval from anyone.

A counselor or faith leader can be a good resource when embarking on inner work, especially for getting an outside perspective on what we think we're learning about ourselves. Everyone is a practicing human being, though, so even a counselor or faith leader could be wholly or partially wrong about you.

You can try reading Carl Jung's works, though many of his writings are heavy going. Perhaps start with the recommendations on this web page: "A Beginner's Guide to Reading Jung" (https://jungiancenter.org/a-beginners-guide-to-reading-jung-2/).

Both Campbell and Jung make much of archetypes, and I agree that archetypes are important. An archetype is a (usually) recognizable image that transcends cultures and time. Some examples of archetypes include the devouring or nourishing mother, the hero, the sage, the magician, the innocent, and many other such universal personality constructs. Campbell and Jung said we all embody and are influenced by archetypes, both those within ourselves and those other people in our lives embody. Archetypes are a type of shortcut, like a symbol, for understanding ourselves and others.

Tarot decks embody universal archetypes, so tarot is a useful tool for exploring your inner landscape. You can use tarot to ask questions of significance, such as "What can I learn about myself from this situation?" The answers can be illuminating, although, as with all inner work, it takes experience, practice, and skill to learn to discern between your hopes, your fears, your wishes, and any truths that are coming your way. If you want to explore this path, here are two books to consider: Rachel Pollack's *A Walk through the Forest of Souls: A Tarot Journey to Spiritual Awakening* (Weiser Books, 2023) and Sallie Nichols's older and somewhat more difficult *Tarot and the Archetypal Journey: The Jungian Path from Darkness to Light* (Weiser Books, 2019; first published by Weiser in 1980 with the title *Jung and Tarot: An Archetypal Journey*).

One fun aspect of tarot is that there is a deck for everyone and every situation. I prefer diverse and inclusive decks, and one of my favorite such decks is the Weiser tarot. Another favorite deck is the Symbolon deck by therapists Peter Orban and Ingrid Zinnel, with art by Thea Weller (US Games). The Symbolon deck can be quite direct in its messages. I once casually drew a card from the Symbolon deck at a friend's request. He asked me to stop talking halfway through my interpretation because he said it was too revealing and accurate. (I don't think he believed I was psychic until that experience.) Opinions are divided on whether the Symbolon is a tarot deck; I lean on the side of it being tarot, because you can find direct associations between the 78 cards in the Symbolon deck and the 78 cards in a regular tarot deck.

While on this journey of doing your inner and shadow work, remind yourself that this journey will continue beyond bodily death, and that any progress you make is praiseworthy and will benefit you for the rest of your immortal existence.

# Chapter 13
# Why do some souls stay in the earthly realm?

As I said much earlier in this book, the first thing that happens after our body dies is that we either speed straight to the afterlife, or someone comes to fetch us and take us to the afterlife. But some souls don't go. Why would someone stay in this existence? The usual reasons are as follows.

- We believe in hell or some equivalent place of eternal damnation and punishment, and when we were in a body, we were so convinced that we are a bad person that we think we're going to hell after our bodies die. Given a choice, we think it's better to stick around in or near our dead bodies rather than go to the hell we expect.
- When in a body, we professed to a belief in an afterlife. We may even have convinced ourselves through the power of denial that we genuinely believed in an afterlife. But we didn't truly believe it, so when our bodies die, we think there's nothing after bodily death and certainly nowhere to go. And because things around us, now that we're in spirit form, look so different from anything we've experienced, or because our beliefs are powerful, we are self-blinded and don't see the way out of this earthly realm after our bodies die.
- We never believed there was any kind of afterlife, so we don't know there's somewhere to go. When our bodies die, we remain, bewildered, blind to any help around us offering to guide us to another existence.
- We think that we are supposed to dissolve into a kind of cosmic ocean where our individuality—everything that makes us who we are—will be gone, and the thought of complete annihilation terrifies us, as it should.
- We are filled with ego, arrogance, and love of earthly power, and even though we know there's more we could move on to, we're afraid we won't feel as powerful in the afterlife as we do on earth, so we stay here.
- We believe that someone still alive cannot survive without us, so we stay on earth to try to run that person's life.

There may be other reasons, but these are the most common. When people remain on earth, they take one of several actions.

1. They possess the body of a living being, usually a human. In the following pages, I call these the possessing kind.
2. They stay in or near their dead body. I call these the bewildered or lingering kind.
3. In one case that I know of, they stay because they don't want to let go of what they see as earthly power. I call this person the arrogant kind.

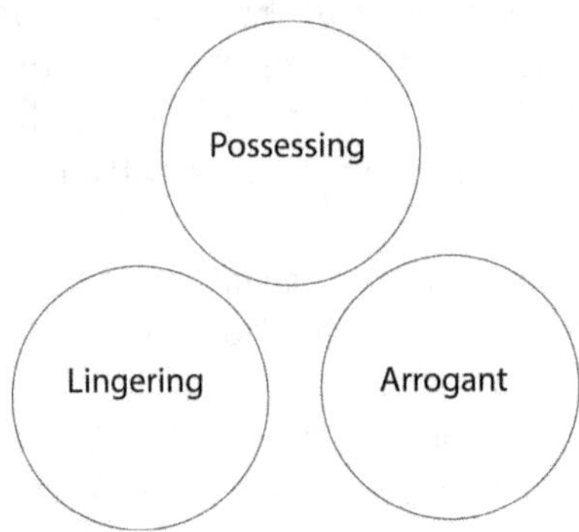


*Figure 37. Three types of lingering souls. Instead of heading for the afterlife, some souls stay on earth and possess others, some linger near their dead bodies (an excellent reason to avoid cemeteries), and one soul I know of hangs around on earth because he doesn't want to let go of his earthly power.*

## *The possessing kind*

Those who stay in this existence can be problematic. The bewildered kind, which I discuss in a bit, usually hang out where their remains are interred. That's okay—eventually they will allow themselves to see the help that's available to them—but what's not okay is that they sometimes try to possess someone's body. (I'm talking about human souls here. Demons are a different and far more difficult type of soul to deal with.)

Normally when I encounter someone who has been possessed by a lingering human soul, I can talk compassionately and rationally with the possessing spirit and convince them to let go. I give them what I call "the talk," the first version of which I got from Edith Fiore's *The Unquiet Dead* (Ballantine Books, 1995). I've since streamlined and modified the talk, and I vary it according to what is needed for specific situations.

When I give the talk, the possessing spirit knows I'm telling the truth because, although it is possible to lie in spirit, it's much easier to discern truth from lies on the spirit level. I've given this speech remotely and in person, and it almost always works.

The talk goes something along the following lines.

"Look, I understand your fear. You think you'll go to hell, or you think you'll vanish out of existence. In all my experiences working with people who have died, I've only ever seen a place you might call heaven. I've never seen anything resembling hell. Everyone goes to heaven. It's filled with infinite justice and mercy. That's the next step on your path."

Quite often, by the time I've gotten that far in my talk, the possessing soul has seen heaven through my eyes, has understood that I am telling the truth, and has booked it for the afterlife. If they haven't left, I continue my speech.

"For as long as you are possessing this person, you are hindering both their spiritual advancement and yours. Neither of you can make any spiritual progress while you are controlling them. There's a lot more to life than the life you led in a physical body, and you can only discover what's next by leaving this person's body and heading on to the next stage in your existence."

Most remaining souls leave when they hear this. I once encountered one stubborn soul for whom these statements were not persuasive enough. I tell that story in a bit.

## *My first depossession experience*

I first learned about depossessing people in an emergency. In 1996, my ten-year-old daughter and I attended my paternal grandfather's funeral in El Cerrito, California. While at the cemetery, my daughter wandered through the outdoor mausoleum, calling out (she later told me, to my horror), "Is anybody here?"

After the funeral, the family convened at my brother Pete's home in Cupertino. I heard a terrible cry from the backyard where my daughter was playing. As I rushed out, I ran past my uncle Raymond Michaels, my biological father's brother, standing with his hands in his pockets looking at my daughter. I've never met Raymond; he died in the Korean War in 1950 and was buried in the same cemetery in which my grandfather had just been buried. And although I'd been communicating with spirits for almost a decade by then, I seldom saw them as a physical presence. Yet I was so focused on my daughter that I didn't think twice of running past a spirit.

Just past Raymond, my daughter was on the ground with a broken wrist. She said some people had picked her up and thrown her onto the concrete pad she was playing beside. My daughter was and is honest, so I never doubted what she said, even though there was no one physically present who could have done it.

Another brother, David, drove my daughter and me to the hospital, where we waited hours for a doctor. While we waited, I asked the Divine that the best possible doctor be assigned to her. I later found that the long delay was because the original doctor who was supposed to tend her was unexpectedly called away, so they called in another doctor. I thought then and still think the change of doctors was because my daughter's wrist required the specialist she got, and she got that specialist because I had asked for help. (Remember that help is always available, but because of free will, it can't be forced upon you. You must ask for it.)

When the doctor finally arrived, she reported that my daughter's wrist was shattered into many tiny fragments. She didn't think it required surgery, but instead she felt she could move all the pieces into the right place. And she did. Luckily, she was skilled in treating that kind of break. The process was brutal for all concerned. David was a treasure; hugely supportive, he talked me through what was going to happen, including lying to me about how serious it was because he could see I was about to faint. He stayed with us until my daughter was discharged.

On the two-hour drive home on northbound Highway 101 just leaving the Sausalito area, I glanced over at my daughter to see how she was doing. To my horror, I saw her face moving, like someone was molding clay into a new face. Although I'd never experienced possession at the time, and knew nothing about it, I immediately knew what was happening. My mother tiger kicked in. I roared psychically at whoever it was to leave her immediately.

The possessing spirits (there were three, including a male banker, a female socialite, and another woman, all from the 1920s and 1930s) rushed over and tried to possess me instead.

Everything went white. I couldn't see anything, and I heard a dull roaring in my ears. The car kept moving forward while I wrestled with these three lost souls. I quickly realized I was out of my depth; I didn't know what to do.

I called out to God in my mind, asking that he lift these spirits up to where he was. As soon as I asked for help, I saw the three souls rising out of me and up into a circle of light (not a tunnel, but a circle, somewhat like a platform), and then they vanished from my psychic sight.

At the same time, my vision cleared so I could see the road again. I glanced over to my daughter, whose face was now hers again. I breathed a silent "thank you" to God.

Since then, I have never allowed her to go near a cemetery, not because I think she'll be so innocent as to invite someone in again (the possessing souls had taken her "Is anybody here?" as an invitation), but because I'm a better-be-safe-than-sorry person. My daughter agrees and also avoids cemeteries.

I don't know who was driving the car while I was wrestling with those souls, but whoever was helping me, they did a good job keeping us alive. A psychic told me in the 1980s that I have powerful spiritual help and that I wasn't ready to hear who it was. I still don't know who, though I have some guesses. I think whoever that help is was driving while I wrestled with the invaders.

Why did those souls harm and try to possess my daughter? Because they were afraid of punishment in the afterlife, they were afraid to leave earth and had hung around the cemetery for decades waiting for a body to possess. You might say they picked the wrong person, though in the end they were taken to the afterlife they had so feared, and I learned some valuable lessons about possession and cemeteries, so there were good endings all around, except for my daughter's broken wrist.

## *Not all souls can be convinced to stop possessing a person*

As I mentioned a little while ago, one time I encountered a soul who was unpersuaded by the talk. Here's that story.

For a few years, I did psychic readings at a high school graduation party (hosted by a high school in Petaluma, California). The six-hour party had various activities in the school gym. The graduating students were given tickets to spend as they liked on the activities. The purpose of these parties was to give the students an alternative to getting drunk that night and potentially winding up in an automobile accident. In one area of the gym were the tarot readers, astrologers, and so on, and one tool-free psychic (me; by "tool free," I mean I don't need to use tools to access information).

The gym was enormously noisy. Many psychics find it hard to concentrate, let alone receive information, in crowded, noisy places, but somehow I can, so I was happy to participate in these events. (I thought I was volunteering, but to my surprise, at the end of the first event, I was paid $150. That was way below my going rate, but the fun that my young clients and I had was well worth it.) Each year I attended, word quickly spread and I always had a long line of students eager to pay their tickets for a 15-minute reading with me.

One young woman I read for was possessed by her late grandmother. I spoke with the grandmother and gave her my usual depossessing speech, but couldn't get the grandmother to budge. A stubborn, self-satisfied being, she thought she knew better than anyone else what was best for her grandchild. I gave the young woman my card and asked her to contact me for further help. She never did, and I wondered for a long time if she was able to pry her grandmother's cold, dead fingers from her mind. When I finally asked psychically if (a) it was okay for me to get further information and (b) whether the grandmother had stopped possessing her granddaughter,, the answer I got was "yes, and yes." Thank goodness.

## *What types of souls possess living people?*

I've depossessed a lot of people, but most of those people were possessed by human souls who didn't know where to go after their bodies died. The possessing souls didn't mean harm, and after they left upon hearing my talk, the harm they'd inflicted started to repair itself.

A few souls do mean harm, but mostly not the human souls. As I discuss in more detail in chapter 7, some of the possessing entities are demons. I've talked many such into leaving a person alone by speaking with compassion to them. A very few human souls are malevolent, enjoy being malevolent, and don't want to leave. The same is true for most demons: they are malevolent and enjoy being that way. Often, when I give the demons the demon version of the talk, they leave the person they're possessing.

Unfortunately, sometimes the person being possessed doesn't want the malevolent being to leave because it makes them feel strong and safe. When such a person clings to the possessing spirit, whether it's a human or demon soul, I can't do much for those people.

### *The bewildered or lingering kind*

The kind of souls who hang out, bewildered, in their dead bodies are easier to deal with than the possessing kind. I usually just need to give the bewildered ones a variation of the talk, and they go. Sometimes another soul comes to escort them, as the story I tell in a minute illustrates.

I first became aware of this sort of soul delay—souls hanging out in their bodies rather than moving on—when at the acquaintance's mother's funeral I spoke of in an earlier chapter. The funeral was open casket and I had a front row seat. As I listened to the eulogy, I watched the mother try again and again to make her body sit up. She would sit up in spirit, but of course her body didn't budge.

I talked to her (mentally, not aloud! I didn't want to sound crazy, and I didn't want to disturb the eulogy) and explained that her body was kaput; no longer operable. I gave her the talk, and after a long while thinking about it, she left.

Another time, I attended a friend's mother's funeral. I didn't sense anything off, but I was also keeping myself psychically closed down during the funeral and especially once we got to the cemetery. (As I discussed earlier, I'm careful at cemeteries because so many souls hang around where they are buried, not knowing where else to go, and are eager to glom onto any living person, especially sensitive ones.)

That night while I was sleeping at my friend's house, my friend's father, who had died some years before, came rushing by and woke me up. He had stopped by to say hello and leave a message for my friend, then told me he was going to collect his wife, who was still in her casket. I had known the family since I was 17, so it's not surprising that the father gave me the message.

A few years later, that friend's sister told me that one of her nieces had also heard their father say he was coming for his wife, but the niece heard that a week before the funeral. The friend's sister and I pondered the timing and decided that, as the sister said, "They call [them] mysteries for a reason!"

Sometimes a soul's body isn't dead, but is so damaged that the soul isn't inhabiting the body. In those cases, the soul is deciding whether to stay or go. I've recently spoken with the soul of someone whose brain was so damaged, doctors declared there was no hope of them living a normal life should they recover.

The soul was aware their body was in bad shape. They said to me they had been hovering near their body and had said to themselves with a bit of wry humor, "This doesn't look good." They were on the fence about leaving because so many people they loved would be sad at their bodily death. After some discussion in which I showed them what I've seen of the afterlife, and in which I assured them they won't lose any relationships they want to keep, they felt much better about leaving.

## *The arrogant kind*

One soul that I know of hangs out in the physical plane because they're arrogant and ego-driven, and had a moderate mastery of their presence while in a physical body. I was psychically informed in 2023 of that soul, who when in a body had a certain kind of international fame. After his bodily death decades ago, he stayed here on earth. (He has quite the reputation, and people in the esoteric, occult, and magical fields either admire him, sometimes to the point of worship, or fear him still.) He whisks around the world, loving the freedom he has as a disembodied soul.

Some people like to claim they are this person's reincarnation. He gets a hearty laugh out of those claims because (a) no soul that has ever incarnated on earth is ever reincarnated, and (b) he gets an ego boost from how many people want to be him.

While in his body, he was powerful and in charge, and he doesn't want to step back from that. He likes being in charge, and he hasn't left the physical plane because he fears he won't be in charge in the next stage of his existence.

Especially, though he won't admit it to himself, he fears the life review and what will come after. He fears he will be punished; he's not nearly as sanguine as he pretended to be while in a body about the consequences of his actions.

But even more than punishment, he fears not being in complete control of himself. He fears being at the mercy of a greater power, and he's not convinced that the greater power is benevolent or wise. Worse yet, he fears that some of the demonic entities he so casually played with in physical life will want to inflict on him a comeuppance if he leaves the earthly plane. Better, in his estimation, to just stick around on earth.

Out of curiosity, on the theory that I was given this information for a reason, I asked what psychological state he's in. The answer I received is that he's in mourning for his life, including many specific incidents, especially related to his mother and the mother of his children. For him to move on, he needs to face not just those feelings, but also his actions, what he's done, and what the consequences for others were of what he did. As well, he needs to voluntarily consult with a wise one who is familiar with the intricacies of divine thought and our greater existence. Once he does those things, he can return to a relationship of wholeness and love with the divine goddess he rejected, reviled, and misrepresented while in physical life.

I've been advised by my inner guidance not to identify this soul or try to help him because it will stir up trouble. Some people will want to contact this soul through me, some will want to refute me, some will want to know how to banish this soul from this plane. To which my answers are no thanks, everyone has an opinion, and it's not my business what this soul does or where he goes. As far as I'm aware, he's not interfering with anyone now. He's divinely loved just as we all are, and eventually he'll find his way.

# Chapter 14
# Don't wait until after your bodily death

When we die, we only take with us two things: what we've made of ourselves as human beings, and the relationships we've created with other people. We don't take our wealth or physical possessions, no matter how dear those are. And we are, as I discuss much earlier in this book, exactly the same person we were when we were alive.

This means that the time is now if you want to improve yourself or your relationships. Don't wait until after your body dies to start being a better person. Don't wait until after your body dies to appreciate people. Yes, you can send them messages and good wishes from the afterlife, but it's hard for souls in bodies to receive or believe those messages. Appreciate the people in your life now. Make amends now. Do and say the things you're thinking now. Start doing your inner work now. Anything you can do now will help others and will speed your progress as a soul.

## *The world shift, also called the ascension, is already happening*

You may have heard people talking in the 1990s about the year 2012 and the belief that some of us would ascend to a newly enlightened state of being that year. There was loose, judgmental, holier-than-thou talk about how the ascension would only be for the enlightened among us, and the rest of us would be left behind. It was a riff on the equally self-righteous Christian idea of the rapture (an idea not in the Christian Bible, but which instead originated in the 1800s). In the rapture, Christians would be swept up into heaven, leaving behind all non-believers to continue to suffer on earth. (The year 2012 was taken from the idea that the ancient Mayan calendar ended in that year.)

In 1996, I was introduced to a nonphysical being who was new to me and of whom I had never heard. I was with my brother Pete and his then-girlfriend Louise, who was a talented psychic herself.

I had been talking with various nonphysical beings for about seven years by then, so I decided to hold a private spirit communication session for Pete and Louise; a kind of open mic session to which I invited beings only of the highest possible light and love.

As I sat in my rocking chair, I felt what I later described as a Niagara Falls of energy pouring down into my body through the top of my head. Louise told me later that I gripped the arms of my rocking chair so hard, my knuckles turned white.

Then the being started talking to me internally, and I started to translate what I was hearing into English words.

First, the being introduced himself as Metatron. I'd never heard the name. I thought maybe it was the name of one of the Transformers, the heroes in an animated children's series, and I wondered why a celestial being would call themselves by the name of a Transformer. (I'm still amused at that innocent misapprehension.)

But no, Metatron was his name. Jesus had told me some years before that he was teaching me how to better communicate with spirits so that I could speak with his, Jesus's, teacher. When Metatron came through, I knew that Metatron was the teacher Jesus had told me about years before.

One of the first messages Metatron gave me was that 2012 wasn't the year things would happen. Instead, he said, 2020 was the pivotal year. Also, he said, humanity wouldn't be swept up off the earth and carried away, nor would we all suddenly become enlightened. Instead, he explained, we were already, in the 1990s, working our way toward a division that would become more evident in 2020, and that 2020 was the definitive decision year for us all.

The world, he explained, is evolving. As we evolve, Metatron said we are heading toward a choice: to either trust or fear each other. "The world" includes earth and all life and other existences on her, including us human beings.

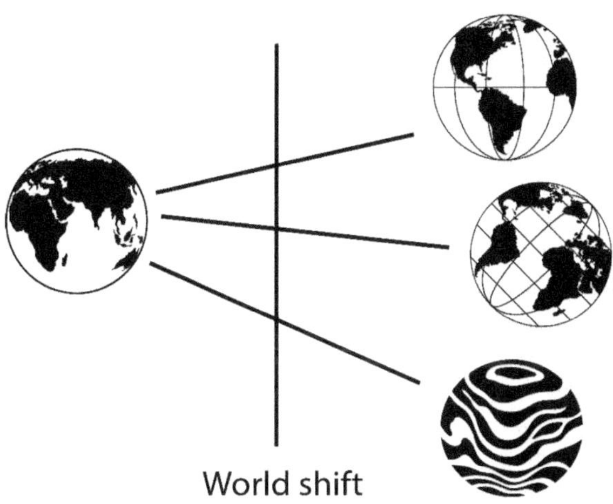


*Figure 38. The process of the world shift is gradual so it doesn't induce fear in humans. Once it completes, there will be an infinite number of earths, each different.*

As the world evolves, we are gradually shifting into the fifth dimension, a dimension in which there are an infinite number of physical realities, including an infinite number of Earths. Because sudden, drastic change can stress us and make us fearful, the process of the world shift is gradual. As the shift happens, we move gently but inexorably further down our chosen paths of trust or fear. The further we walk those paths, the harder it becomes to see those on the other path.

To choose a path, we don't need to be either 100 percent trusting or 100 percent fearful—that's not possible. It's more a matter of degree. If we lean more of the time, even 51 percent of the time, in the direction of trust, that's our choice and our path. If we lean more often in the direction of fear, that's also our choice and our path. Metatron offered no judgment for either path, though I believe that the path of trust is better.

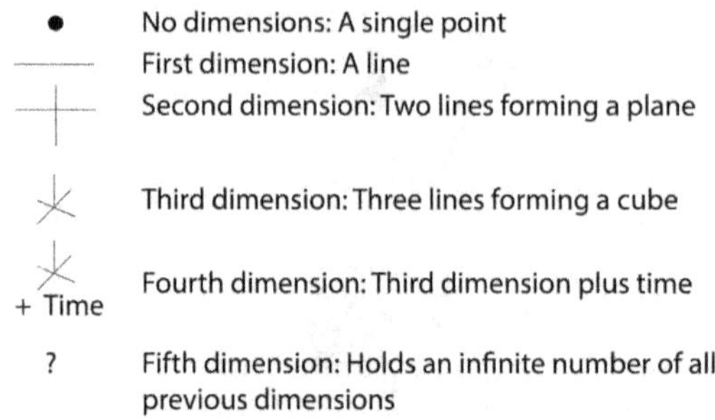


*Figure 39. The first five dimensions. Each dimension contains an infinite number of the previous dimensions within itself.*

Metatron told me in 1996 (and repeated many times over the years since then) that starting in 2020, the choice to be made between trust and fear would gradually become much more obvious and clear to everyone. Eventually, he explained, the world will split into infinite versions of itself as it fully arrives in the fifth dimension. Our choices will influence which version of Earth we end up on. We'll each end up on a version of the world that most suits us. (I've glimpsed some of these possible worlds, and some of the worlds based in fear are horrific. Please choose trust, folks, not fear.)

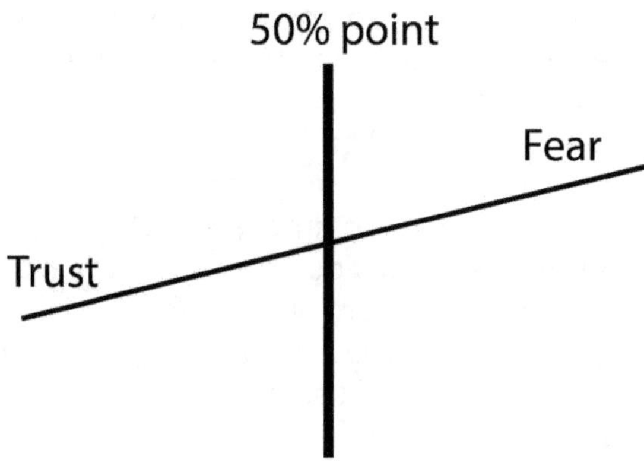


*Figure 40. Aim for more than 50 percent trust; the percentage matters. Think of it as a seesaw on which trust outweighs fear.*

When Metatron first told me about this change, I translated the term he used into the phrase "world shift into the fifth dimension." At the time, others in the New Age field were talking about us all ascending into the fourth dimension. In the late 1990s, I wrote a blog post explaining why it would be a world shift, not an ascension, and that it would be the fifth dimension, not the fourth. In the decades since, I've seen others now referring to the fifth dimension instead of the fourth, so either my post had an effect or others eventually learned more about dimensions. I will never know because, like in many fields, many people are unwilling to give credit where credit is due. Instead, they claim credit for other people's ideas. (And are in that manner choosing fear over trust. They're afraid that if they say they got an idea from someone else, they won't be respected, but the opposite is true: When people find out a person has taken credit for something not their own, people lose respect for the person who took undue credit.)

The shift has been and continues to be gradual so we humans can get used to it, but it's accelerating. At first those of us on either side of the divide will still see each other, but as the shift progresses, the rift between the two choices widens, and we see those on the other path less and less until they vanish from our sight entirely.

It would have been nice if Metatron had warned me about COVID-19, but he didn't. He just told me many times that 2020 was a crucial year in humanity's spiritual development. Over the years, Metatron's messages about this world shift and humanity's part in it often reminded me of what the philosopher and mystic Pierre Teilhard de Chardin said more than 100 years before: That we humans are evolving not just physically but spiritually as well.

The relevance of this information is that it is never too late to make a different choice. If you know you're on an undesirable path, you can change your direction.

Some people want to think their religion is the only true religion and that everyone who worships differently is wrong. I disagree with that way of thinking. It holds you back in your trek up the mountain of becoming because, thinking that way, you won't be open to different viewpoints, and you may be condemning and rejecting people simply because they believe, nonharmfully, in something different than you do. And, in case it isn't obvious, that kind of belief is a choice for fear, not trust, and I doubt you want to go where that choice will take you.

## *Things unseen are still real*

I once had a friend I dearly loved, but from whom I'd been receiving some confusing treatment over the years. I had sometimes tried speaking with her about her behavior, only to be met with denial. Eventually, I withdrew from the friendship; not completely, but enough to be a relief to me. The friend noticed and asked why, but I didn't answer, having learned that nothing I said would make a difference.

A few months later, the friend's then-recently departed aunt came to me and encouraged me to say something to that friend about why I had withdrawn so much from our friendship. After hesitating a few months, I spoke up to my friend, only this time I was more direct rather than gently circumspect. But again I didn't see that my words had an effect. I asked the aunt if I needed to say it again.

The aunt replied, to my surprise, that there was no need. She went on to say, "You've done enough and more than anyone else was willing to do or has done. You no longer need to say anything more."

I asked her, "Have my conversations had any positive effect on her?"

"Yes," the aunt said.

"I'm surprised," I said. "I don't see any such effect. How have I helped?"

She said, "**Things unseen are still real**; your mercy and compassion and above all honesty and courage in confronting her affected her on a deep level, and will help her in the afterlife, when she can no longer lie to herself or deny things. What you said will have no effect while she is alive, but they're invaluable to her after she moves on from the physical world."

The point I take from that statement is, you may never see it, but your actions have consequences. We can draw from that statement a summary of this book, too. We as souls continue forever and shouldn't let ourselves stagnate. Instead, we can always be striving to improve ourselves and, as needed, helping our fellow human beings.

After our physical body dies, we all go to the afterlife, which is a loving, non-judgmental place. Therefore, it's never too early or too late to start making a better person of yourself. As John Steinbeck said in *East of Eden* (Viking Press, 1952), "And now that you don't have to be perfect, you can be good." All your actions affect others around you. Being dishonest affects others around you, even if you think you got away with the deception. When you act out of compassion and honesty, your actions affect others. That's a better direction to go in.

Believe in yourself, trust yourself and all of life, and speak up when you need to. If you feel the impulse to say something, and, after examining yourself, are sure that impulse is coming from a loving place, have the courage to speak. Your actions may have no obvious or immediate result, but they will do good.

And if a sincere, honest, reasonable person remembers you doing something harmful to them and wants to talk about it, listen to them. It doesn't matter whether you remember it. There's a saying, "The axe forgets; the tree remembers." That saying means that the person doing the harm, whether inadvertently or on purpose, is the axe and forgets the harm they've done, but the person they harmed, the tree, remembers. If you, the axe, don't remember, give them, the tree, the benefit of the doubt and apologize sincerely, regardless of whether you did it intentionally or even if you remember doing it. An apology hurts no one and can help enormously.

In doing all these things, you're modeling behavior to those who need that modeling. You're planting seeds that will grow. Make sure you're not planting weeds, but instead are planting life-affirming and life-supporting seeds.

Things unseen are still real.

# Appendix A. Terms and territory

I wasn't raised with any religion, and consider myself a mystic, very similar in beliefs to those of Charles Williams, though not quite so Church of England as his beliefs were. Throughout this book, I use terms like god, gods, goddess, and goddesses; the Divine; soul and souls; heaven and hell; prayer; and other spiritual and religious terms. I use these terms because they are the easiest way to convey the idea of what I see and who I communicate with in ways that will make sense to most people.

The terms I use all have equivalents in other religions and belief systems. Their meanings should be self-evident to you, but in case they aren't, I'll talk a bit about them in this chapter, along with the concept of beliefs about reality and reality itself, for which I use the analogy of a map (our beliefs about reality) versus the territory the map represents (reality).

## *Terms used in this book*

Here, I briefly discuss what some terms I use mean to me. Feel free to substitute your own terms when encountering a term you don't use.

For the most part I refer to **the Divine** throughout this book rather than use terms like god, goddess, or specific Divine names. "Divine" encompasses much of what I perceive the god/goddess/creator of all things to be. The terms is gender neutral and conveys the idea of the multiplicity of the being who is all things and everywhere.

I refer to **soul** and **souls** to represent who we are. We are souls inhabiting physical bodies; we don't "have" souls, and our souls aren't (and can't be) separate from who we are.

**Heaven** is a term for a reality beyond physical reality. It's a place we all go after our physical bodies die. How it appears to us varies according to our preferences and beliefs; there is no "one size fits all" afterlife and there is definitely no restriction on who goes to the afterlife. We all go to the afterlife, no matter what we've done in physical reality.

**Hell** as a place of eternal punishment into which non-believers of various religions are cast doesn't exist. There is a place I call the outer darkness. For details, see chapter 8.

**Prayer** is a way to communicate with the Divine. None of the divinities I've spoken with has bad intentions toward us. None has ever said they need to be worshiped or supplicated and definitely not sacrificed to. Instead, they have all said they would like to develop a personal relationship with each of us. The best way to do so is to simply talk with them, which you an call prayer if you wish, though I reserve the word "prayer" for when I have a request of them. Otherwise, when I talk with a Divine being, I call it a conversation or a spirit communication, if I'm feeling like being fancy with my terms.

## *Our map of reality is just that—a map, not reality*

Although my beliefs are individual and formed from my experiences and what I've been told by non-physical beings and by the great Infinity of reality, I don't make the mistake of thinking my beliefs *about* reality are reality. I believe we all exist in a greater reality that some of us glimpse parts of sometimes. I encourage you to be your own authority and to not be constrained by others' ideas, even mine.

Here is an analogy I like to use to explain what I mean: the mental maps we make of reality are representations of reality; they aren't reality itself. Many people have heard the phrase, "the map is not the territory." For those of you who haven't heard this, or who have heard this but wondered what it means, it means that just as a road map is not the territory the map shows, our ideas about reality aren't identical to reality. Here's an analogy explaining what that means.

Imagine you hike through some lovely mountain areas. Following a faint path, you cross some streams, you see some boulders and trees and a meadow. You see a lot of wildlife.

Now let's further specify that you take this hike in spring.

As you travel through the area in spring, to share the wonder and excitement of your hike, you draw a map showing where the streams, boulders, trees, and meadow are. You mark where you spotted a herd of deer, a fox, a badger, some trout in the stream.

When you return from your journey, you share your map and your enjoyment of the territory you traveled with others. Some of those you share your map are excited by your experiences and return to the same mountains hoping to have the same experiences you had.

But let's say those you share with don't visit in spring. Instead, they visit the mountains in autumn when the streams have dried up, the meadow is no longer filled with flowers, the deer have moved to lower pastures, and maybe some boulders were pushed downstream in a spring flood after you visited. Furthermore, these later visitors might notice different things, and they may see things you missed, or they may later misremember what they saw.

*Figure 40. The map you create of the reality you experience is unique to you. Others may experience the same reality similarly, but not identically.*

The map you drew in spring was only a single snapshot in time and was based on what you noticed and your memory. It's still useful as a general outline of where things are, but it isn't the reality of the mountain. It's not useful as an accurate representation of what another person will experience.

If you and the people you shared your map with are aware that the map is not reality but is instead a rough guide, everything is okay.

But as soon as you start to insist that your map is the only reality and that anyone who experiences anything differently is wrong, you mislead yourself and others. This confusion of map for territory is a big factor in disagreements and religious wars.

## *Beliefs don't cancel other beliefs*

I've seen a lot of things that aren't what other people believe. Everything I've seen and experienced has been filtered through my ideas, beliefs, education (formal and informal), and experiences. My beliefs are an eclectic mix that boils down to respecting all life, which includes what most people consider inanimate or non-living. When my experiences and reality differ from what other people believe, I don't think those experiences and beliefs invalidate other people's realities, nor do I think that other peoples' experiences invalidate mine. (Sometimes people feel challenged or insecure if someone has different beliefs and experiences than they do.)

For this reason, I don't talk about a lot of the things I know (or think I know) unless they are relevant. Depending on the person and context, I exercise this restraint for a few reasons. The main reason is this: when it's clear that someone isn't open to new ideas, it's kind and polite to not expose them to those ideas. My only exceptions to this are when someone's ideas are leading them to harm other people, or when my intuition tells me that saying something might help them in some way at some time in their lives. Then I speak up.

Like everyone, I have opinions that I formed out of evidence and thought, and like any honest, rational person, I can change my mind with further evidence, just as I did with my beliefs about reincarnation, which went through a number of sea changes before arriving at my present beliefs.

I know my beliefs about reincarnation don't explain everything, and I know there's a lot more to learn. So keep in mind that what I say in this book is my thinking today; it may change. And I'm okay with that. I don't need to know precisely how reincarnation works to operate in my daily life, and what I already know has been helpful to many of my clients (and to me).

My beliefs are useful, and they'll be more useful the more I expand them to incorporate new information. Sometimes the contradictions and unclarities are themselves the source of further learning. For example, I once idly wondered, "What happens after heaven, and how can there be souls who have evolved beyond being human souls, especially since I don't see those souls in heaven? How does that fit in with reincarnation?" I instantly got an answer (which I give earlier in this book). I don't believe it's the complete answer, but it perfectly filled in some gaps in my beliefs.

## *Be your own authority*

Our beliefs about reality are exactly that—beliefs *about* reality. Those beliefs aren't reality itself. No matter what we believe, those beliefs are a tool we use to navigate reality. Just as we can change tools to suit our needs, we can change our beliefs if our beliefs aren't working for us. I encourage you to think about what you believe and ask yourself where those beliefs came from. If you believe something because someone else told you to, is that belief a life-affirming, positive one that serves you and those around you? One that makes life better for everyone? If not, you can change it.

Keep this in mind as you think about what you've read in this book. I've related what I've experienced as a medium, psychic, and spirit communication specialist through the terminology of my beliefs. If something I say doesn't fit your beliefs, you are free to adapt what I say to what you believe, or to change your beliefs a little bit or a lot, if what I relate opens new perspectives for you.

# Appendix B. Annotated bibliography

This appendix contains an annotated list of the books and resources mentioned in this book. Because I find it interesting, the dates given for each book are mostly the original publication date. Many are still in print and you can often find later publications of the same book.

Alighieri, Dante. *The Divine Comedy*, first published in 1320, translated by Dorothy Sayers. *Part 1: Hell*, Penguin Classics, 1950. *Part 2: Purgatory*, Penguin Classics, 1955. *Part 3: Paradise*, Penguin Classics, 1962. These books are among the best English translations of Dante's work. (Some Spanish and Portuguese translations come closest to retaining the original Italian metrics and rhyme.) Dante's views of heaven and the Divine coincide greatly with what I've seen firsthand as a psychic. John Ciardi's translation of *The Divine Comedy* (W. W. Norton & Company, 1961), which I quote from in chapter 12, is also excellent. As a side note, Dorothy Sayers also greatly admired and deeply understood Charles Williams' work. I first mention Dante in chapter 2, and then at times throughout the book; most quotations are from the Sayers translations.

Amorth, Gabriele, Society of Saint Paul. *An Exorcist Tells His Story*, Ignatius Press, 1999. Father Amorth worked as an exorcist for many decades. His stories have much deep truth about the nature of demons, and describe some approaches to dealing with demons that I disagree with. Mentioned in chapter 7.

Amorth, Gabriele, Society of Saint Paul. *An Exorcist: More Stories*, Ignatius Press, 2002. Mentioned in chapter 7.

Anderson, Nathaniel E and Kent A. Kiehl. "Psychopathy: developmental perspectives and their implications for treatment. *Restorative Neurology and Neuroscience*, 2014 (https://pubmed.ncbi.nlm.nih.gov/23542910/). Discusses psychopaths and how, if caught young enough, it's possible that psychopaths' behavior can be mitigated. Mentioned in chapter 12.

Berne, Eric. *Games People Play: The Psychology of Human Relationships*, Grove Press, 1964. Berne teaches a theory of interpersonal relationships based on transactional psychology. This book is a bit hard to read now, but popularized the idea of people playing social and mental games with each other—what those games are, how to recognize them, and how to move those games into a more adult, responsible, honest form of communication. Mentioned in chapter 6.

Berne, Eric. *What Do You Say After You Say Hello?*, Grove Press, 1969. Berne describes life scripts—patterns of interactions with others that we repeat. We create these patterns to get approval from our parents, especially our mothers, and continue those patterns throughout life or until we resolve our issues. Mentioned in chapter 12.

Boone, J. Allen. *Kinship with All Life*, Harper & Row, 1956. Boone spends half the book describing his relationship with Strongheart, a German Shepherd famous for his movies in the 1920s. Boone's premise is that all living things have an intelligence and are souls incarnating in physical bodies. In his book, Boone tells of how he communicated with Strongheart and later with other living beings, such as a fly. Mentioned in chapter 8.

Campbell, Joseph. *Hero with a Thousand Faces*, Pantheon Press, 1949. A popular work that's been in print for decades. Campbell focuses on the archetype of the hero. We see this archetype throughout myth and legend and in many books and movies. Mentioned in chapter 12.

Campbell, Joseph and Bill Moyers. *The Power of Myth*, Doubleday, 1988. Joseph Campbell made a name for himself talking about the importance of myth and archetypes in our everyday lives. Countless screenplays use his hero's journey as a basis for their stories. This book is a more accessible version of Joseph Campbell's theories. Mentioned in chapters 2 and 11.

Carter, Les. "Surviving Narcissism," a series of gentle, compassionate YouTube videos on narcissism—what it is (and isn't), how to recognize it, how to deal with a narcissist, and so on. Mentioned in chapter 8.

Church, Dawson. *Mind to Matter: The Astonishing Science of How Your Brain Creates Material Reality*, Hay House Inc., 2018. Describes results from tests showing how we can alter our brain's electrical field to affect our health and the health of those around us. Mentioned in chapter 4.

Dickens, Charles. *A Christmas Carol*, Chapman & Hall, 1843. A classic Christmas story about a traumatized man who inflicts his trauma on everyone around him until late in life, when three spirits visit him on Christmas Eve and show he can still change. Mentioned in chapters 5 and 11.

Durvasula, Ramani. YouTube channel titled "DoctorRamani." This channel has many videos on narcissism—what it is (and isn't), how to recognize it, how to deal with a narcissist, and so on. Mentioned in chapter 8.

Dyer, Wayne. *Pulling Your Own Strings*, Funk & Wagnalls Co, 1978. A popular and useful text on how to recognize that you aren't a victim and instead have choices. Mentioned in chapter 12.

Ehrman, Bart D. *Forged: Writing in the Name of God—Why the Bible's Authors Are Not Who We Think They Are*, HarperOne, 2011. One of many books by many scholars showing how Biblical texts were altered and outright forged in ancient times. Mentioned in chapter 7.

Elgin, Suzette Haden. *The Gentle Art of Verbal Self-Defense,* Barnes & Noble Books, 1993. Elgin teaches how to recognize when we are verbally attacked (by the phrase "If you *really* loved me" and other such phrases) and teaches how to respond to those attacks. Mentioned in chapter 6.

Engle, Beverly. *The Emotionally Abused Woman: Overcoming Destructive Patterns and Reclaiming Yourself*, Ballantine Books, 1992. A short, useful book on how abuse can be emotional, focusing on how such abuse looks like for women. Mentioned in chapter 10.

Eurich, Tasha. "Working with People Who Aren't Self-Aware," https://hbr.org/2018/10/working-with-people-who-arent-self-aware, October 19, 2018; retrieved September 8, 2024. Mentioned in chapter 4.

Fenton, Ferrar. *The Holy Bible in Modern English, translated from the original Hebrew, Chaldee, and Greek Languages*, Destiny Publishers, 1966. First published in 1903. Rather than translating from existing translations, Fenton translated the Hebrew and Christian Bibles from original sources, and consulted with contemporary Jewish scholars to get the most accurate translation he could. (An action that some of his contemporary Christians found repugnant.) Ferrar comments in his introduction that he was surprised at how many things that were in existing translations were not in the original texts, and at how many things that were in the original texts were missing from existing translations. The translation of the standoff between Moses and the Pharaoh is particularly interesting. Mentioned in chapters 2, 7, and 8.

Fiore, Edith. *The Unquiet Dead*, Ballantine Books, 1995. Describes how the dead can possess the living, and how to convince the dead to leave the people they are possessing. Mentioned in chapter 13.

Foor, Daniel. *Ancestral Medicine: Rituals for Personal and Family Healing*, Bear & Company, 2017. Teaches an approach to working with ancestors. Mentioned in chapter 10.

Frankfort, Henri. *Ancient Egyptian Religion: An Interpretation*. Columbia University Press, 1948. Frankfort talks about ancient Egyptian myths and offers some new (for his time) perspectives, in particular on the concept of Ma'at. Mentioned in chapter 12.

Geddes, Linda. "Fear of a smell can be passed down several generations," https://www.newscientist.com/article/dn24677-fear-of-a-smell-can-be-passed-down-several-generations/, retrieved October 26, 2024. Discusses how a fear of a smell can be passed down through several generations of mice, with the assumption that the fear is passed along genetically. This research implies there could be similar fears and attitudes passed down genetically through human generations. Mentioned in chapter 10.

Golden Earring. *Radar Love*, 1973. A popular song about how two lovers can communicate across space without a physical method. Mentioned in chapter 2.

Goulston, Mark. *Just Listen: Discover the Secret to Getting Through to Absolutely Anyone*, Amacom, 2015. Goulston describes approaches you can take to talk with just about anyone. Mentioned in chapter 7.

Graves, Robert and Raphael Patai. *Hebrew Myths*, Doubleday, 1963. Gathers and translates many pre-Biblical myths and shows how those ancient myths were used in the Hebrew Bible. Mentioned in chapter 7.

Heller, Joseph. *Catch-22*, Simon & Schuster, 1961. A fictional work describing the insanity of war. Mentioned in chapter 7.

Hendrickson, Nancy. *Ancestral Tarot: Uncover Your Past and Chart Your Future*, Weiser Books, 2021. Hendrickson teaches how to use tarot to connect with your ancestors and through those connections, gain insight into yourself and into family characteristics, including generational trauma. Mentioned in chapter 10.

Hendrickson, Nancy. *Ancestral Grimoire: Connect with the Wisdom of the Ancestors through Tarot, Oracles, and Magic*, Weiser Books, 2022. A second book by Hendrickson on using tarot to connect with ancestors. Mentioned in chapter 10.

Henwg, Taliesin (534-599 CE). "The Battle of Goddeu" (also known as "The Battle of the Trees"). https://www.ancienttexts.org/library/celtic/ctexts/t08.html (accessed December 26, 2024). This Welsh poem's topics include life, existence, and reincarnation. Mentioned in chapter 8.

Horn, Mark. *Tarot and the Gates of Light: A Kabbalistic Path to Liberation*, Destiny Books, 2020. Leads readers through the annual, introspective, 49-day Jewish/Kabbalistic practice called Counting the Omer, connecting each day of counting to the Kabbalah and to the associated tarot cards. When Kabbalah is spelled with a K, it refers to the Jewish tradition. When spelled with a C, it refers to the Christian variation of the Jewish version. When spelled with a Q, it refers to the Hermetic variation of the Jewish version. Mentioned in chapter 3.

Jung, Carl. *Aion: Researches into the Phenomenology of the Self*, second edition, Princeton University Press, 1979. Considered one of Jung's master works, *Aion* is not for the faint of heart. Read only after you've read other of Jung's works recommended by the Jungian Center for the Spiritual Sciences (op. cit.). Mentioned in chapter 12.

Jung, Carl. *Visions: Notes of the Seminar Given in 1930–1934*, Princeton University Press 1997. Notes from a seminar Jung gave focused on the inner experiences of a woman Jung worked with. Mentioned in chapter 12.

Jungian Center for the Spiritual Sciences. "A Beginner's Guide to Reading Jung," https://jungiancenter.org/a-beginners-guide-to-reading-jung-2/, retrieved September 28, 2024. A guide for those new to Jung on which works to read in which order. Mentioned in chapter 12.

Kübler-Ross, Elisabeth. *On Death and Dying: What the Dying Have to Teach Doctors, Nurses, Clergy and Their Own Families*, Scribner reissue edition, 2014. Dr. Kübler-Ross brought to greater attention the necessity of facing and dealing with death rather than being in denial about it. She also introduced the concept of the five stages of death: denial and isolation, anger, bargaining, depression, and acceptance. Mentioned in chapter 11.

Le Guin, Ursula. *A Wizard of Earthsea*, Parnassus Press, 1968. A popular fiction book set on a multicultural planet where magic exists. Mentioned in chapter 4.

Michaels, Marina. "Channeling: A German General Speaks," http://thelighthouseonline.com/channel/jan23_96.html. Material received from Rudolph Hess from his perspective in the afterlife. Mentioned in chapter 8.

Michaels, Marina. *The Forgiving LifeStyle: How to Forgive Everyone (Including Yourself)*. Athena Star Press, 2014. Describes an easy three-step process for forgiving others, and explains why forgiveness is important to you. Mentioned in chapter 12.

Michaels, Marina. "Seth on Healing Energies." Material received from Seth about the nature of healing. https://thelighthouseonline.com/channel/Seth_on_energy.html. Mentioned in chapter 8.

Miller, Alice. *The Drama of the Gifted Child*, revised edition, Basic Books, 1997. Alice Miller was one of the first psychologists to urge her fellow psychologists to pay attention to what children say about their childhood experiences, rather than always assume that there was nothing wrong with the parents and that the child (who might now be an adult) was just complaining. Mentioned in chapter 12.

Miller, Martin. *The True "Drama of the Gifted Child": The Phantom Alice Miller — The Real Person*, independently published, 2018. Martin Miller, Alice Miller's son and also a psychologist, reveals his struggle with a mother admired by everyone but who was abusive to him. Mentioned in chapter 12.

Nichols, Sallie. *Tarot and the Archetypal Journey: The Jungian Path from Darkness to Light*, Weiser Books, 2019. (First published by Weiser in 1980 with the title *Jung and Tarot: An Archetypal Journey*.) An older and somewhat more difficult book, but one of the best, on Jung's ideas about tarot and archetypes. Mentioned in chapter 12.

Nietzsche, Friedrich. *Beyond Good and Evil: Prelude to a Philosophy of the Future*, C. G. Naumann of Leipzig, 1886. Nietzsche had a rather grim view of humankind and life, yet he also had many thought-provoking things to say. Mentioned in chapter 12.

Pessoa, Fernando. "Palco de vida" ("Stages of Life"). Text quoted in full here: https://murderiseverywhere.blogspot.com/2017/06/on-being-happy-debunked-papal-homily.html (retrieved December 18, 2024). The words are often falsely attributed to a Catholic pope. There's no proof Pessoa wrote this, nor is there any proof he didn't. The words are encouraging and wise nonetheless. Mentioned in chapter 12.

Pollack, Rachel. *A Walk through the Forest of Souls: A Tarot Journey to Spiritual Awakening*, Weiser Books, 2023. A masterwork on how the individual tarot cards represent myths, legends, archetypes, and psychological truths. Excellent for those using tarot for inner work. Mentioned in chapter 12.

*The Pope's Exorcist*, 2023. A movie based on the experiences of Father Gabriel Amorth, an exorcist for the Catholic pope. Mentioned in chapter 7.

Pratchett, Terry. *Reaper Man*, NAL, 1991. A fictional novel about Death personified and his encounters with a group of cosmic beings called the Auditors. One of the 41 books in Pratchett's Discworld series, which I highly recommend. Mentioned in chapter 7.

Reid, Jay. *Growing Up as the Scapegoat to a Narcissistic Parent: A Guide to Healing*, independently published, 2023. One of the best descriptions of a narcissistic parent from the point of view of a child scapegoated by such a parent. Mentioned in chapter 8.

Saint Teresa of Ávila. *The Life of St. Teresa of Jesus: The Autobiography of Teresa of Ávila*. Saint Teresa was a Carmelite nun in the 1500s. Mentioned in chapter 12.

Schucman, Helen. *A Course in Miracles*, Foundation for Inner Peace, 1976. A set of books received as dictation from Jesus by a Jewish psychologist. It's about forgiveness and hope and viewing a perfected world; about how we all have God's love and help. Mentioned in chapter 12.

Shakespeare, William. *As You Like It*. A play possibly written in 1599. It's since been performed many times and adapted to radio and films. Mentioned in chapter 9.

Shakespeare, William. *Hamlet*. A play written sometime between 1599 and 1601. Like *As You Like It*, Hamlet has been performed many times and adapted to radio and films (and is one of my favorites). Mentioned in chapter 1.

Steinbeck John. *East of Eden*, Viking Press, 1952. A long book filled with much wisdom. Mentioned in chapter 14.

Tutu, Desmond and Mpho Tutu. *Made for Goodness: And Why This Makes All the Difference*, HarperOne, 2010. Desmond Tutu was a South African Archbishop; his daughter Mpho Tutu van Furth is a South African priest. Mentioned in chapters 4 and 12.

van der Kelk, Bessel. *The Body Keeps the Score: Brain, Mind, and Body in the Healing of Trauma*, Penguin Books, 2015. Backed by scientific research, the author shows how everything we experience, especially emotional trauma, is stored in our bodies, and gives guidance on how to heal, at least in part, from that trauma by working with our bodies. Mentioned in chapters 6 and 12.

*What Dreams May Come*, 1998. A movie starring Robin Williams. The movie represents a fairly close approximation of what heaven is like as I've seen it. Mentioned in chapter 2.

# Index

## Numbers



## A

# B



# C

# D

# E



# F

# G



# H

# O



# P

# Q



# R



# S

# T

# U



# V



# W



# Y



# Z

www.ingramcontent.com/pod-product-compliance
Lightning Source LLC
LaVergne TN
LVHW050622100826
845148LV00011B/1700

* 9 7 8 1 6 0 0 3 8 0 1 3 6 *